A LOT TO REMEMBER

CALAIS

BOULOGNE

LE TOUQUET

0   50   100   150   200
KILOMETRES

ABBEVILLE

TANCARVILLE
LE HAVRE   ROUEN
PONT-
AUDEMER
BERNAY   ANET
L'AIGLE   PARIS
ABB° DE LA GRANDE TRAPPE   SEINE

BELLÊME
LA FERTÉ-BERNARD
LE MANS   St CALAIS   CHAMBORD
MONTOIRE   BLOIS
LE LOIR   VEUVES   CHAUMONT
TOURS   AMBOISE
CHENONCEAUX
LOIRE   SAUMUR   AZAY DE RIDEAU
ABB° DE   CHINON   LOCHES
FONTEVRAULT   INDRE   LA CHESNAY
CHÂTEAUROUX
ARGENTON
CREUSE   ALLIER   LOIRE
LYON

LIMOGES

LE PUY
PÉRIGUEUX   VÉZÈRE   BRIVE   ARGENTAT
DORDOGNE   AURILLAC   AUROUX
ENTRAYGUES   MARVEJOLS
Gd VABRE   ESPALION   MENDE
BORDEAUX   FIGEAC   ESTAING   St GENIEZ D'OLT
CONQUES   RODEZ
MARMONDE   LOT   CAHORS   VILLEFRANCHE-DE-ROUERGUE
VILLENEUVE   MONTPELLIER-LE-VIEUX
SUR-LOT   AVEYRON   TARN   MILLAU
AGEN   ALBI   AVIGNON
GARONNE   TOULOUSE
BÉZIERS
CARCASSONNE
FOIX

A LOT TO REMEMBER

*A Supernatural Journey
Through the French Province
of Lot*

by Joan Grant

ARIEL PRESS
Atlanta, Georgia

This book was made possible
by anonymous gifts
to the Publication Fund of Light

ISBN 0-89804-160-0

Contents

To
Denys and Charles
with Love
for
A Lot To Remember

Introduction

Joan Grant's first book, *Winged Pharaoh*, was published in 1937 and instantly became a bestseller. She placed a period of history within the immediate grasp of the reader. It was impossible to escape the impression that the author had, in fact, lived the life of her main character. The following eight books only confirmed this unique talent. But these books were generally regarded as fiction, based on meticulous research.

Joan—once one has met her it is difficult to think of her by any other name—was content to let this appraisal ride until 1957 when she published *Time Out of Mind* (also known as *Far Memory*). This was the autobiography of the first thirty years of her life and culminates in an account of how *Winged Pharaoh* was written. Only then did the general public learn that it was not a novel based upon research at all. It was the story of a former lifetime of hers which she had recalled by virtue of a faculty she named Far Memory.

Of the nine Far Memory books, the story of *Winged Pharaoh* takes place in the first Dynasty of Egypt; that of *Eyes of Horus,* which is continued in *Lord of the Horizon,* in the Eleventh, and that of *So Moses Was Born* in the Sixteenth. *Life as Carola* concerns Italy during the Renaissance and *Return to Elysium* relates a life in Greece and Rome during the first or second century B.C. *Scarlet Feather* is the memory of a life as a member of a tribe of North American Indians at a time before there was any reliably recorded history. It is perhaps of interest that while subsequent archeological finds have corroborated certain details in these stories, no scholar in any discipline has ever discovered an anachronism in them.

The *Scarlet Fish and Other Stories* and *Redskin Morning* are collections of stories which were told to Joan during other childhoods. She set herself to remember them for the benefit of the children she was caring for during World War II. *The Laird and the Lady (Castle Cloud)* is her only work of pure fiction. But more about the books later—this is primarily a note about their author. To have met Joan in anecdotal mood is to wish she had written a second volume of autobiography. As it is, a brief outline must suffice.

Joan was born in 1907. Her mother was a psychic and her father a man of such intellectual brilliance, especially in the fields of Mathematics and Engineering, that he was appointed a Fellow of King's College, Cambridge whilst still in his twenties. So Joan's heredity was in her favour.

From early childhood, she flashed on memories of previous lives and took it for granted that these earlier lifetimes were part of her personal experience. However, any mention of them was met with the same kind of shocked disapproval that greeted an announcement that she wished to go to the lavatory or knew how babies were born. So she assumed that to say anything about what had happened to her before her birth as Joan was just another of those things that was not done. It never occurred to her that not everyone possessed the faculty.

On Armistice night in 1918 she learned the truth. She was permitted to attend the celebratory dinner party her father was giving at the Criterion Restaurant which used to overlook Piccadilly Circus. As she watched the crowds dancing in the streets below she remarked, "Thank goodness, Billy and Max and the others can be born again now without being shot." Her mother's response was, "My dear child, none of those ridiculous stories tonight, please!" And it was only then that Joan realized with astonishment, "But they don't remember...!"

Far Memory was not Joan's only strange faculty. The outbreak of war in 1914 was the start, for seven-year-old Joan, of a most harrowing period. Night after night, in her sleep, she would find herself on the battlefront in France ministering in one way or another to the newly dead and the dying. One of these experiences received verification.

One morning Joan came down late for breakfast and found a young man in khaki by himself at the table. Joan said to him, "Somehow I know that you will not laugh at me. Last night I was with a man called McAndrew when he was killed. I can describe the regimental badge though I cannot remember the name of the regiment, except that it was not an English one. And I can tell you the slang name of his trench."

The young officer did not laugh. Instead, he identified the regiment from Joan's description. It was Canadian. Soon afterward he wrote to Joan's father. "For heaven's sake don't laugh at the child. I cannot attempt an explanation, but I have checked what she said. A battalion of that regiment went over the top on a night attack a few hours before she told me about it at breakfast. A private called McAndrew was among the killed. She was even correct about the local name of the front-line trench."

Joan's formal education was limited to what she absorbed from a series of governesses. She feels she learned far more from the after-dinner conversations between her father and his fellow-scientists.

When Joan was in her teens her father resolved to devote his brains and much of his fortune to ridding Hayling Island, where he lived, of its mosquitos. The project involved not only drainage schemes on a large scale but intensive study of the creatures themselves, both in the laboratory which he built in his own house and in the field.

This work led, incidently, to the founding of The Mosquito Control Institute and the definitive monograph on the insect. It was illustrated with microphotographs taken by her father on a camera of his own devising, for the technique was barely in its infancy.

In all this, Joan was his assistant. She is no stranger to the scientific method. In fact she has a very practical side. She has an uncanny knack of getting straight to the crux of a problem in most areas of her life. It is rarely that she does not find an ingenious, workable solution. She also found time to become a golf champion.

When she was twenty, Joan married Leslie Grant, by whom she had her daughter, Gillian. This marriage ended soon after *Winged Pharaoh* was published and her life with Charles Beatty, who became her second husband, began. Charles, nephew of the famous Admiral, was a philosopher and a visionary. He was the author of several books including *The Garden of the Golden Flower,* a treatise on the psychiatrist Carl Jung.

When Charles was invalided out of the Army he took Joan to Trelydan, his family estate in North Wales. There, throughout the war, they kept open house and gave boundless hospitality to wives and families whose husbands were on active service. In addition, people arrived or were sent from all over the country for help with psychological problems. It was during this period that Joan began to appreciate that certain problems stemmed from experiences which had occurred during a former life. They were yet accessible to therapy, though this was only one aspect of her psychotherapeutic technique.

Her work so impressed Dr. Alec Kerr Clarkson that he used his considerable influence and obtained a grant to establish what was to have been called 'The Bionomic Research Unit', to be run by Joan, Charles and himself. Alas, he died before the project could be started. Joan and Charles never charged anyone a penny for their services and hospitality. Joan continued to write other Far Memory books, *The Laird and the Lady,* and *Vague Vacation,* which derived from a brief holiday in France in 1947. In 1949 financial circumstances compelled them to leave Trelydan.

They settled in The Albany, just off Piccadilly. Charles became the Food Consultant to Fortnum and Mason while Joan, on behalf of the same establishment, embarked on a new and highly complex operation, rapidly freezing the dishes prepared by the top French restaurants and importing them into England.

In 1956 they moved to Ireland for some months where Joan wrote *Time Out of Mind*. When this book was completed, the publisher, Robert Hale, comissioned her to write a book about her favourite region of France, the valley of the river Lot. Several months of 1957 were spent in that area gathering the material which forms part of *A Lot to Remember*.

By the end of 1957 it had become apparent to both Joan and Charles that certain differences in their personalities were irreconcilable and in May 1958 Joan and I met for the first time. I feel that this meeting was an example of what Jung called 'Chronicity.' My experiences in psychiatry during the preceding ten years had equipped me in perhaps a unique way to recognise the therapeutic potential in Joan's talents. Events moved swiftly. In July of that year we began living and working together and in 1960 we were married. In 1966 we co-authored *Many Lifetimes*, which is an account of our work and thinking up to that point.

Joan's revelations concerning Far Memory precipitated controversy that still persists. They were not merely accepted, but were welcomed with relief by a surprisingly large number of people who found their own secret beliefs validated. Others judged them to be escapist fantasies, whilst a few held the faculty to be pure fraud.

But personal feeling about the nature of Far Memory is irrelevant to appreciation of the books, for they stand firmly on their literary merit. In addition to the detail of the daily life of the time and place which gives them such an uncanny sense of immediacy, they have a certain very special quality. Throughout her life—Joan would say with conviction, "Throughout her many lives"—she has been preoccupied with the subject of ethics. By this she means that fundamental and timeless code of attitudes and behaviour to one another on which the health of the individual and of society depends. Each book explores a facet of that code. The First Dynasty of Egypt once knew the code well, but lost it and foundered. Eleven dynasties were to pass before it was recovered, but those were more leisurely times when the most lethal weapon was an arrow, a javelin or a club. We feel that in the present troubled days of this planet these books must be preserved.

Denys Kelsey
October 1979

A LOT TO REMEMBER

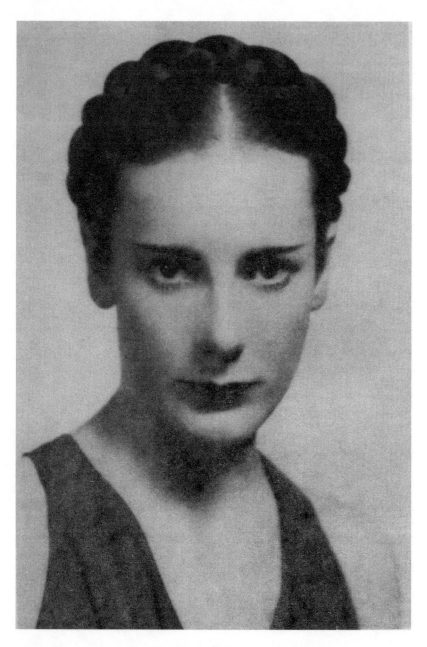

Joan Grant

Chapter One
TO THE LOIRE

As I write this opening chapter, which I can now do as the rest of the manuscript is finished, it is difficult to decide whether it should be listed as Travel or as Autobiography. The action takes place between 1956 and 1960, with flashbacks to 1938, and is shared by Charles Beatty, while I was married to him, and by my husband, Denys Kelsey. The locale is the Lot—rhyming with 'Hot' instead of with 'Lo', as in 'Lo and Behold'— a French department of some three thousand square miles, and the river Lot which rises in the Massif Central, the lower vertebrae of the body of France, and loops westwards until it joins the Garonne sixty miles southeast of Bordeaux.

The book was conceived while I was sitting despondently on a mildewed haystack in County Wexford, watching Prosper, a king-sized springer spaniel, chasing his crow. It could properly be described as 'his' crow, for he had chased it for weeks before it toppled off a branch into his mouth, an accident which caused him to bring it home so that he could guard it devotedly from my six-toed cats while it convalesced in his basket.

I knew that Prosper would be content to chase his crow, day after day, week after week: but how much longer could I endure watching hounds chase foxes? For five long months I had been in Ireland, among a redundancy of horses and far too many hostile spooks. It had been bearable because I was fully occupied with writing *Time Out of Mind,* the autobiography of my first thirty years as Joan, which described how I trained the faculty of 'far memory' up to the time when I wrote *Winged Pharaoh.*

But now it was finished, so what was I going to do with myself? Today at least it was not raining, but the thin April sunshine gave only the illusion of warmth. If only there were real heat to bake the winter from my bones! After wallowing in similar woebegone thoughts I suddenly decided that providence must be prompted to transfer me to a more congenial climate.

Three days later I was flying from Dublin to London, where providence, in the person of Robert Hale, to whom I shall be eternally grateful, provided the means, in advance royalties, for Charles and me to find ourselves, within a fortnight, on our way to the Lot.

As this was a second visit, and I have since been there twice with Denys, this book follows a topographical rather than a chronological sequence, so as to provide a route, for those whose time is limited, which would give a fairly comprehensive view of the Lot in a holiday of two or three weeks.

Being a confirmed map-addict, I would rather find myself in a noble cellar without a cork-screw than in France without Michelin's large scale series; so, I strongly advise getting at least Michelin numbers 75 and 79 before following factually in my tracks.

Also get the current *Guide Michelin,* because although the town plans in an out-of-date edition might still be useful, the recommended hotels and restaurants may have changed hands and so had their rating altered or deleted. This is heartfelt advice, for Denys and I made a long detour to lunch at Rodez, as we had done the previous year when we enjoyed a meal as memorable as the one described in Chapter 26, and discovered too late that the gastronomic genius of Madame Fraux no longer presided at the station buffet.

By car to Brive, the chief town of the region where recollections of the Lot begin, is 400 miles from Le Havre, and I prefer this overnight crossing from Southampton instead of arriving later in the day at Boulogne, or at Calais which adds seventy miles to the journey, for the early start allows a leisurely drive before a night on the Loire. Alternatives are the air-ferries to Calais, or Le Touquet, or taking the car by train from Boulogne to Lyon as we did, in reverse, on our way home.

So when Denys and I left his consulting-room in Harley Street on 28th April, 1960, his appointment book for the following day had a single entry: '20.00 hrs. Southampton Docks!' We had expected to cross on the *Normania,* and so were surprised to see *St. Patrick* on the stern of the ship alongside Dock 7. I was not only surprised but startled, for I recognized her as the elderly vessel who had conveyed me through a Force 9 gale from Fishguard to Rosslare. As we boarded her there was no doubt she was the same ship; a little more battered, a little shabbier, with even blacker smoke belching from her stack to rebuke with smuts the boastful freshness of paint on nearby ships. But there was a great change for all that: the bar shelves were bare of bottles, incongruous as a wake without a corpse.

A glum steward conducted us to our stateroom with its private bath—there are two of these on the channel-boats which do the overnight run and they are a luxury which at times can be worth immeasurably more than the extra charge of thirty-five shillings—and I saw it was unchanged since Prosper had been the cause of my sleeping in it. When the Purser had told me that dogs were not allowed in the cabins I had replied that I should have to spend the night with Prosper in the kennels.

"Do you take me for the kind of man who would dream of subjecting a lady to such inconvenience?" he had said indignantly, and had insisted that we occupied Stateroom A with the grand creature without paying an extra penny for the privilege.

But why were the bars no longer flowing with Guinness and Irish whiskey? Circumloquaciously the story emerged from members of the crew. This was the *St. Patrick's* first run to France, she having been sold away from her own sea and being no more than a stand-in for the *Normania* who was temporarily engaged on a cruise. As if this were not sorrow enough, an officious customs officer, he English of course, had noticed that the seal on the bond cupboard was broken and had refused to allow a drop of anything to be sold until every bottle on board had been rechecked. From the Purser downwards, everyone assured me that this operation would be over in a matter of minutes—ten, at the very most.

Minutes congealed into an hour before the sparse group of thirsty passengers went gloomily to wash down their Irish dinner with water. We fared slightly better, for my reminiscence of the superb seamanship which had remained unruffled even when four hundred milk-churns broke adrift in the forward hold to add their clatter to the storm's cacophony, caused us to be directed to the third-class bar, where we were stealthily revived by glasses of the 'real stuff', Paddy's Three Swallows.

Fortunately the voyage was as smooth as my previous one in her had been turbulent, and the sun was shining when we disembarked at Le Havre, having breakfasted at leisure while more impatient characters hurried off the boat, unaware that this misplaced energy would gain them nothing except a wait in the draughty customs shed.

By eight o'clock we were following N.182 along the foot of the chalk cliffs, white as marguerites in the early light, which bastion the Seine until well above Rouen. The road surface was bumpy until we reached Tancarville, having been broken up by the heavy traffic during the construction of the suspension bridge which for the first time we could cross instead of having to wait for the ferry. The road on the other side was smooth as a bowling alley and we were through Pont Audemer and at Bernay in less than another hour. Instead of taking N. 138 to Le Mans, as we would have done had we been going by *grandes routes* via Tours and Limoges, we took a more direct line across country, for the map-addict seldom likes travelling by main roads.

The verges were quilted with cowslips and the poplars copper bright between flowering apple orchards, a prelude to an abundance of asphodel in the Forêt de la Trappe. The asphodel was a far more pleasing sight than the famous Trappist monastery, which looks more like a prison than a venerable abbey.

After an excellent lunch at the Boule d'Or in Belleme, we stopped at la Ferté-Bernard to photograph the twin towers of the fifteenth-century town gate, but did no more than stare dutifully at the façade of Notre Dame des Marais, having long since decided that a surfeit of sight-seeing is more unwise than ingesting a rich *paté* when already replete.

By the time we reached St. Calais we felt sufficiently nimble to get out of the car to admire the carving on the doors of the church, which gave me the excuse to inform Denys that St. Calais is the birthplace of Charles Garnier, the son of a wheelwright, who was the architect of the casino at Monte Carlo and the Paris Opera House. We crossed le Loir at Montoire, the relatively undistinguished river from which the *départment* Loir et Cher is named, and came to la Loire at Veuves, a hamlet between Amboise and Blois.

We had intended to spend the night in Blois, not to revisit the château, nor the *Son et Lumière,* moving as this is, at the Château de Chambord, but so as to experience again the superb *terrine maison,* the succulent pigeons or some equally delicious dish at Chez Léon, a restaurant I had originally discovered, not in the *Guide Michelin,* but through the kindly advice of a garagist.

Charles and I had had a magnificent, hilarious and startlingly inexpensive lunch there, at a table shared by an elderly couple who first became endearing by complimenting me—and Charles's accent—on having been so discerning as to marry a Frenchman. A few mouthfuls later they were sharing with us their sorrow at Madame's recent miscarriage, a notable event as they had been married for forty-three years. His right leg had been amputated at the thigh in a casualty clearing station during the first years of the Kaiser's war. But this wound, so Madame assured me, had in no way diminished her beloved husband, and they had embarked on another child, which would have been thirty years younger than the others, only to prove to their patronizing grandchildren that the old people were still fully conversant with the joys of the bed.

Denys and I had an equally good, though less anecdotal lunch, when we went to Chez Léon, but we did not stay in Blois for when we saw the Château de Chaumont, serene on its wooded height beyond the lucent river, we decided to look for a hotel in the little town threaded below it at the water's edge. Even before I had finished nest building, a process which usually includes arranging flowers we have collected during the day—a vase and a two-litre milk-can to keep them fresh being essential items of our equipment— the view of the Loire flowing gently below the bedroom windows made us agree that it would be foolish not to prolong our stay, should we also approve our dinner. And the dinner was worthy of the *alose,* a delectable species of shad which we had never eaten before, because it comes upriver only in early summer. So it was three days later when we reluctantly left the Hostellerie du Château.

Chapter Two
THE FAMILY OF FRANÇOIS PREMIER

The valley of the Loire is no more than a prelude to the Lot, but here the vision begins to widen and the centuries to unfurl their banners. There are more facts in the history of its illustrious châteaux than there are notes in a symphony, but I will offer a stave from the tune, as an errand boy may whistle a theme from Mozart.

The principal actors on this stage belong to the sixteenth century, and so are contemporary with our Tudors; but while Henry VIII and his three children, Edward VI, Mary Tudor, and Elizabeth I, ruled England, there were three, instead of two, generations of the French royal family. Its progenitor, François I, the 'François Premier' whose name runs life a leit-motif through the spiel of nearly every château guide, lacked none of the magnificent flamboyance of Henry Tudor, nor was he a less exuberant patron of the renaissance of the arts. Did Henry, one wonders, revere Holbein as François revered Leonardo da Vinci, who was the only man in France in whose presence the King respectfully took off his hat.

François was far more fortunate than was Henry with women. He opined that 'A Court without women is like a year without Spring, or a Spring without roses', perhaps because he was born with two women kneeling at his feet'. These women were his wise and loving mother, Louise, Countess of Angoulême, and his sister, 'the Marguerite of Marguerites', who married the King of Navarre.

His first queen was his cousin, Claude, so kindly a woman that she deserves to be remembered for more than giving her name, *reineclaude,* to the plum we know as a greenage. She was lame, like her mother

Anne of Brittany, whose oratory at Loches has an intimate perfection which shows that she did not feel it needful to set a cohort of clerics between herself and her gentle god.

Many were Anne's prayers for a son in whom Brittany and France would be united, but these prayers were not answered. She had no children by her first royal husband, Charles VIII, that estimable young man who died after hitting his head on a low doorway while hurrying to play Jeu de Paume at Amboise, the game which is the ancestor of lawn tennis and still called the Game of Kings; and as the queen of Louis XII she had only one daughter, Claude.

Louis XII had divorced his first wife, Louis XI's daughter, Jeanne of France, in order to marry Anne. It was a marriage of expediency, but he became so devoted to her that when she died his tears were considered embarrassingly excessive for a royal mourner. However, at last he dried them, and took for his new bride Mary Tudor, the sister of Henry VIII, who in every respect differed from Henry's daughter of the same name, often prefixed with 'Bloody'.

François, who was the heir to a sickly old man and married to that old man's daughter, cannot have relished the prospect of welcoming his new stepmother-in-law—as Mary already was, having been married to Louis in England by proxy—but he arrayed himself in 'cloth of silver and gold, with a cloak of white silk thrown over his shoulders' when he went to meet her at Abbeville. He must have known that she was only sixteen, but he certainly did not expect her to be ravishingly lovely. Her red-gold hair! Her sparkling eyes! What might these not kindle in the feeble King?

One can well imagine François's anxiety when, on the morning after the wedding night, a radiant Louis announced to his astonished courtiers 'I have worked miracles!' For the next two months he continued to report his amatory progress in such phrases as 'I am in

22

tremendous fettle!' or 'I am in really magnificent form''
But then his vigour proved to have been the last
flickers of a dying fire, and he took to his bed, to wait
in it alone for death.

Death kept Louis waiting for five months, during
which time Mary caused a fresh crop of anxieties to
arise in François. He discovered that for two years she
had been in love with Suffolk, the English ambassador
who had accompanied her from England. François
appealed to his mother, who briskly told Suffolk that
should he donate a Dauphin to France, she and her son
would become joint Regents, and their first act would
be to send the baby's papa in disgrace back to England.
Suffolk must have been greatly relieved that the French
view of queenly infidelities was so much less stringent
than that pertaining at the court of his royal master,
where he would have lost his head literally instead of
receiving fifty thousand livres from the kindly Countess as compensation for her having forbidden him to
lose it again figuratively.

François, who since infancy had been loved and
loving, was in no way a jealous man and sincerely
sympathizedwith Suffolk, for by now he too had fallen
in love with Mary. So that his rival should not feel
neglected, Françoise arranged for his favourite mistress to keep the Englishman happily occupied.

However, the Countess now took a firm hand in the
domestic arrangements. Realizing that her son was
only too likely to provide the heir which would lose
him his kingdom, she decreed that Mary was to share
Claude's bed until Louis died; a simple solution to the
problem whic continued until Mary was widowed, on
New Year's Day, 1515.

Yet even then François was not sure of his throne, for
Mary pointed out to him that, as she did not feel
inclined to swear on oath that there was no possibility
of her being pregnant, he must wait the prescribed
forty days before he could be certain that she was not

carrying a posthumous child. During this period she was guarded day and night, by two ladies at a time, behind the barred doors and shutters of the Hôtel de Cluny. The anxieties of François increased. for it was reported that each day the Queen grew a little fatter. Rumours that she was *enceinte* spread throughout France, throughout Europe; until the Countess discovered that Mary was only teasing them by wearing each day an additional layer of under garments.

Again François proved the goodness of his nature, for instead of being furious, he did his best to persuade Mary to marry him, even though this would have entailed divorcing Claude of whom he was fond. But Mary prettily declined his pressing invitation again to become the reigning queen of France: instead she retrieved Suffolk from his temporary nesting place, took him back to England and married him.

The Game of Kings was again to play a part in changing history, as it had done when an earlier Dauphin was foolish enough to send a basket of tennis balls to Henry V, implying that he was more familiar with the use of them than he was with balls designed for cannon—for the eldest son of François drank a glass of water while over-heated after playing tennis, and shortly expired in agony. Some historians are of the opinion that the water had been poisoned at the behest of his sister-in-law, Catherine de Medici; but experience of the after-effects of drinking water in French villages suggests that there is no need to take so dramatic a view.

So when François died in 1547, he was succeeded by his second son, Henri II, who was so different in character to his father that neither of them was ever able to understand the other. Henri never overcame the bitter resentment he felt at having been sent to Spain to replace his father as a hostage, after François had been captured at the Battle of Pavia, which was fought on Italian soil.

Henri was fourteen when at last he returned from the arid formality of the Spanish Court. He was shocked to find a gay father surrounded by adoring women, and François was no less dismayed to meet a son who had become priggish and uncouth and even spoke French with a strong accent. Instead of nagging the boy, François again displayed his innate understanding by putting his son under the care of Diane de Poitiers. She was twenty years older than Henri and one of the most beautiful and cultured women of her generation. Under her gentle tutelage at her château of Anet, he became less withdrawn, less boorish, and then fell passionately in love with her, and she with him; a devotion that increased throughout their lives.

One can well understand his resurgence of bitterness against his father when he was told that he must marry the Pope's niece, Catherine de Medici, who had nothing to commend her except enormous riches. To make matters worse, she was plain as well as bourgeoise, and he thought she had not even the wit to realize that the Court ladies referred to her, behind her back, as the Goldsmith's Daughter. For years he refused to play his part in providing an heir to the throne, until Diane at last managed to persuade him that he could no longer avoid this distasteful duty.

Throughout Henri's reign, Diane, except by legal title, was his beloved queen, while Catherine was little more than the incubator of his progeny. This service she performed eight times, on the last occasion being delivered of twins who failed to survive infancy. With the exception of her third son, later to become Henri III, for whom she had a devastating devotion, she saw her children only as pawns in the battle of power, religious and political, for which she had been ruthlessly trained since early childhood. She had been deliberately conditioned by the Medicis to regard any form of human affection as a degrading weakness—a devil's distraction from blind obedience to the dictates of

Church and State. Her father, in order to be able to assure the Pope that she was an instrument well tempered to their purposes, had even gone to the lengths of poisoning her favourite lap-dog, and forcing the child to watch without displaying any emotion while it slowly expired in agony.

This was only one of the means by which Catherine was taught how to close her heart against any trace of affection, so it is not surprising that all her children were deficient in physical, mental or spiritual health. In the eldest son, François, this defect showed itself only through bodily symptons, a lesser handicap due no doubt to his good fortune in being brought up by Diane de Poiters, so that he could be educated with the child he was to marry, whom his father had already put under her benign aegis. This child was Mary Stuart, who, when she came to France at the age of four, was already Queen of Scotland in her own right. François and Mary loved each other dearly, but their idyllic childhood, with its background of Diane's châteaux of Anet and Chenonceaux, came abruptly to an end when a lance splintered at a tournament in Paris.

The broken lance jerked upwards, forcing open the visor of the royal tilting helm, and a splinter pierced Henri's right eye. In an attempt to assess the extent of the brain injury, surgeons pierced with similar splinters the eyes of four criminals from the Chavet prison, freshly decapitated for the purpose; but any information they may have gained proved ineffective for in four days the King died.

Catherine the wife had been queen only in name: Catherine the widow, through her children, ruled a darkened France. Her religious fanaticism was at first disguised as political necessity, as when, in the courtyard of Amboise, Huguenots were slaughtered on the pretext of conspiracy, while the appalled François and Mary were forced to watch. Catherine had the corpses festooned from the balconies of the château, perhaps

26

to demonstrate that her nerves were much stronger than those of her son and his wife, who had fainted at the dreadful spectacle; but although she did not fear her victim's ghosts, the stench of rotting flesh soon caused her to move the Court to Blois.

François II, when under the protection of Diane, had been comparatively healthy, though never robust. But Mary was not old nor wise enough to shield him from his mother's implacable demands on his slender resources, and in 1560, after reigning less than a year, he died, and the crown passed to Charles, his brother.

Charles IX was prey to delusions of persecution and to maniacal outbursts of sadistic rage. His Court soon became known as 'The most dissolute Court the world has ever seen'; but although his strange amusements could only be factually described in a textbook of psychiatry, he tried to check his mother's fanatical hatred of Protestants until she at last managed to coerce him into giving the order for the holocaust which is usually referred to as The Massacre of Saint Bartholomew. It began at six o'clock in the morning of 24th August, 1572, and by midday over two thousand corpses littered the streets and quays of Paris, and even the corridors of the Louvre itself. Charles, no doubt feeling that this crusade was getting too close for comfort, gave orders for the killing to cease. There was a lull—but only a lull. The following morning monks appeared in every district of the city proclaiming that a hawthorn tree had burst into unseasonable bloom in the Cemetery of The Innocents and that this 'miracle' was a sign that God wished the massacre to continue. So a lot more Protestants were killed by Catholics with even greater enthusiasm.

Two years later Charles IX died, to be succeded by his unpleasant brother, Henri III. Catherine, who could steel herself against every other source of fond emotion, could deny him nothing. When he happened to feel like dressing as a woman she provided the clothes, and paid for the banquet or masque at which her darling could shine. One wonders which guest, after one of these parties at which Henri, with diamonds in his violet powered hair, wore a robe of rose and silver damask, its sleeves embroidered with gold thread and clusters of emeralds, was brave enough to comment that the bodice, moulded over an iron corset, was cut so low that...

> *Chacun estoit en peine*
> *C'il voyait un roi-femme,*
> *Ou bien un homme-reine.*

Henri might have developed more benignly had his mother not deliberately thwarted his only spontaneous drive towards a normal outlet for affection. At the wedding of his sister Margot to Henri of Navarre, the grandson of François Premier's sister Marguerite, he fell passionately in love with Marie, wife of the Prince de Condé. To remove him from the girl whom Catherine saw only as a rival, she arranged for him to leave France to become the King of Poland. However, instead of forgetting Marie he became even more determined to marry her, and the moment he succeeded to the throne he set about trying to arrange her divorce. The proceedings were held up because Marie was pregnant: and she died giving birth to a daughter.

Henri fell into a delirium of grief which crossed the borders of sanity. Skulls were embroidered on his doublets, and at Avignon, during Christmas week, he donned the habit of a monk to lead a torchlight procession for hours through the streets while young courtiers, stripped to the waist, lashed each other with whips until the blood spurted from their bodies in an orgy of masochistic mourning.

It is probable that among these youths were Henri's bodyguard of favourites, the *Quarante-Cinq Mignons* as they came to be called, 'Those fearsome painted and pomaded bullies, dressed in open-necked doublets, leg-of-mutton sleeves, tight-fitting trunks and skin-tight hose', to quote from Jean Duché,* to whom I am indebted for much of the information in this chapter. The *Mignons* flattered and fawned on Henri, and they also murdered for him. Their most famous victim was the Duc de Guise, one of the most popular men in France, whom the people had affectionately nicknamed the 'King of Paris'. He was a great man even in stature, being all of six foot six, and it took the combined efforts of several *mignons* to kill him; but at last he died, spouting blood like a fountain from a dozen or more dagger wounds with his fist thrust into his mouth so that he should not cry out.

Catherine, who was also in the château of Blois, was still in bed when Henri went to tell her what he had done, boasting that now he was not the King of France but the King of Paris. She knew that at last he had gone too far, and that Madame Serpent, as the people called her, could no longer control or protect the viper she had hatched. She made a 'terrible grimace and fell back in despair, and eleven days later the last of her strength had ebbed away and she was dead'.

Had she lived for another eight months she would have seen the son on whom she had lavished such a dreadful wealth smother-love excommunicated for de Guise's murder, and then assassinated in a particularly humiliating manner, by being stabbed in the pit of the stomach by a pious Dominican monk, Jacques Clement, to whom he was granting audience while seated on the commode.

Catherine's son-in-law, Henri of Navarre, who had married her daughter Margot, then became Henri IV. Like his great-uncle, François Premier, his amatory laurels remained green to the end of his reign, and earned him the affectionate soubriquet of the 'Vert Gallant'.

* *The History of France,* as told to Juliette, Burke, 1958.

Chapter Three
PHANTOM PRISONER

While Denys and I were at Chaumont, we visited the château and were suitably impressed, except by the guide's assertion that the room which communicates with Catherine de Medici's bedroom—her bedroom also has a door leading to the gallery of the chapel—was the personal apartment of her astrologer. She frequently resorted to purveyors of prophecies and poisons, but I very much doubt if she did so openly, and it is much more likely that she used the adjoining room as a boudoir—the word is derived from the French *bouder*, meaning to sulk—where her consultants in the darker arts could approach discreetly by a private stair.

After her husband's death, she gave Chaumont to Diane de Poitiers, in exchange for Diane's favourite château of Chenonceaux. This is usually considered to have been an act of deliberate malice, but I think it probable that Diane preferred to leave the place which was so poignantly associated with her years of happiness with her royal lover. She is supposed to have been virtually a prisoner in Chaumont, but in fact she stayed there only six weeks and then returned to her château of Anet,* on the Eure, where she is depicted in high relief over the gateway in the guise of the goddess Diana embracing a stag.

At Chenonceaux we found the vast parterre planted with a profluence of pansies, tens of thousands of them in violet-blue or yellow, a masterpiece of bedding-out

*The house and gardens of Anet can be seen only on Sundays, Thursday afternoons and public holidays. The gateway is on the main road, N.828, 10 miles north-north-east of Dreux.

which must have needed an army of gardeners although there was not a single one in sight. It would be
tempting but illusory to imagine the lovely Diane
gazing down at the limpid waters of the Cher from a
window of the wing which spans the river, for this
wing was added by Catherine. The most likely ghost, if
in fact the place was haunted, would be Louise de
Vaudemont, the docile little widow of Henri III, who
lived there for eleven years wearing the white mourning of queens, which caused her to be known as The
White Lady.

We had lunched, very indifferently, at Amboise, and
then visited the château, mounting to the upper terrace by the spiral ramp which takes the place of a
central stairway and was designed so that the royal
retinue could ascend without dismounting from their
horses. It was a very hot day and by the time I reached
the top of it I wished that I either was, or had, a horse.
However, the view from the great terrace is well worth
the climb, and on the ramparts is the exquisite little
chapel built by Charles VIII for Anne of Brittany. It is
in this chapel that Leonardo da Vinci's bones have
been re-interred; or the bones presumed to be his,
which were found under the ruins of another chapel
within the castle walls in which he was originally
buried. It is from here that the guide points out the
manor of Close-Lucé, a gift to Leonardo from his royal
patron, but it has been drastically restored, and only
the chapel remains as he knew it.

I enjoyed this second visit to Amboise much more
than I had enjoyed my first, which was in midwinter
when ice was stampeding down the Loire in ochre
slabs, which groaned and creaked together under my
chilly bedroom window until it was only too easy to
imagine that the sound was an echo of Huguenot
corpses twisting and turning in the dark wind. But that
was before Hitler's war and has no place in this story,
so I will go back only four years, to the time when

Charles and I came to the Loire on our way to the Lot.

We had intended only to spend the night at Langeais, fifteen miles downriver from Tours, but the cooking at the Restaurant Duchesse Anne was so excellent, the Family Hotel to which it belonged so comfortable, that we decided to linger. It was probably this mood of happy greed which causes me still to see Azey-le-Rideau as rising lightly as a soufflé from its swan moat. To reward Charles for also going cheerfully round Villandry, Blois, Chenonceaux and Langeais, we then went to Saumur—not to see the château but so that he could drink at its place of origin one of his favourite wines. After lunch we left the town by D.145 for the forest of Fontevrault, in which solomon's seal was plentiful as bracken in an English wood; and glades were carpeted with lily-of-the-valley. Fontevrault would have remained for me no more than a pleasing setting in which to walk off lunch, if we had not come to a high, forbidding wall where a notice beside a pair of enormous iron gates curtly ordered: *'Sonnez la Guide!'* On a sudden hunch I obeyed; to regret it a moment later when one of the doors opened to reveal a sinister man in the uniform of a prison warder.

I attempted to retreat, which made him look even more surly. And I was still wondering how to convince him that I was not trying to smuggle a hacksaw to an incarcerated chum by the time he was locking and barring the doors behind us. We were now in a tunnel which, so thick were the outer walls, could easily have garaged a double-decker bus.

"You will wait here until another warder comes to show you round," announced our gaoler. "Visitors are not allowed to circulate except under strict surveillance."

The last thing I wanted to do was to see round a prison, and I said so. His eyes became even more glacial. "You must have wanted to see round the abbey. Otherwise, why did you ring the bell?"

Before I could reply, he withdrew to his lair in the side of the tunnel, slammed the door, and stood staring malevolently through the barred window. A notice informed us that we were in the precincts of an abbey founded at the end of the eleventh century, in which for seven hundred years, until Napoleon turned it into a civil prison, a community of both monks and nuns was ruled over by an abbess. Beyond the tunnel there was an open space of gravel flanked by curved walls, and at the far side a steel door in an even higher one. I crossed it to look at three rose bushes, but they were not cheerful either, being smothered with green-fly. So we sat disconsolately on a plank bench in the shade of the tunnel, until after about a quarter of an hour, Charles rapped on the door of the gaoler's lair and asked how much longer we were expected to wait.

The door opened a couple of inches to vent: "Twenty minutes—perhaps longer—do not be impatient!"—and then slammed shut again before we could use the delay as an excuse to escape.

I was far more uneasy than circumstances justified. I told myself that I was restless only because I was bored. But my feeling intensified, until I had to admit that there was a spook in the immediate vicinity. A spook in a French prison seemed only too probable, and it was the last thing I wanted to see. In an attempt to tune it out I counted the paving stones, did sums in my head, tried to remember the numbers of all the roads we had been on since Havre; but none of these evasions were any use.

Reluctantly I had to accept the fact that something, or someone, who five minutes ago had been outside my range of perception, was relentlessly coming into focus....Now I could see three dead men lying on the gravel near the right-hand wall. There was another man on the ground near them; but he was not dead, for he was trying to crawl. I could smell blood, and cordite—and fear. The stench of fear was sickeningly strong.

With an effort I jerked myself back and said urgently: "Get me out of here or I'll be sick!"

Charles is usually more than willing to help me dodge spooks, but he said that he felt there was a job here which urgently needed doing. He already had a notebook open on the bench beside him, so I knew I must have been talking aloud instead of only seeing in silence. Trivial fears, of being sick in public, of being arrested as a dangerous lunatic by the warder, of returning to find myself being stared at by a crowd of giggling tourists, dwindled as I accepted someone else's much deeper fear which I must try to do something about.

I shut my eyes, and started to see what had happened immediately before the men had been killed. But the scene was still impersonal, as though I were watching a coloured film. I could hear myself talking, but it sounded unreal, as though it were being played back on a tape-recorder...

"I can see four prisoners—French prisoners. One of them is quite young; the others are middle-aged; but none of them is the ghost. With them is a German guard, a boy of nineteen, with yellow hair and pale blue eyes. He is afraid of the prisoners, although he is armed with a machine-pistol and they have only wooden rakes. They are raking up straw and shavings which fell from the lorries, the lorries which unload here...

"The Frenchmen are whispering to each other; loud whispers which they intend the German boy to overhear. They describe what will happen to Germans when the town is liberated. The boy tries to ignore them. He wants to shout at them to be silent; but he knows that to do so would betray his fear. He is becoming hysterical with fear. A muscle is twitching in his left eyebrow. But none of the Frenchmen realize they are driving him too far for their own safety...

"Suddenly he shrieks at them to be silent. They grin

34

and go on raking the gravel. The gritty sounds of their raking are the only sound. Then they start whispering again. The boy's voice is shrill with fear as he shouts an order at them. Suddenly one of the Frenchmen laughs. In panic fear the boy lets off the gun. It jerks in his hand; I can feel it jerking. The gun has become part of him, as though the bullets spurting out of it were a physical release from unbearable tension...

"The body of the last man to fall is gaping open, as though it had been cleft with an axe instead of by bullets. The German boy is whimpering like a dog in pain. Three of the prisoners are dead, but the youngest is trying to crawl away, dragging himself along on his elbows. Both his legs are broken. The boy turns the gun on him but does not fire it. Perhaps there are no more bullets....

"The boy shot himself that night. He was to be court-martialled for exceeding his orders. But that was not why he killed himself....He killed himself because he thought he was a coward—a coward who feared whispers....

"Pray for the soul of a German who killed Frenchmen here....Pray for the soul of a German who killed Frenchmen here...."

"Joan! Come back, Joan!" Charle's urgent voice brought me back with a jerk. I sat up and saw the warder unlocking the gates to let in a party of tourists.

"I think he killed himself on the twenty-fourth of July, 1944," I said dazedly. "I am quite certain of the rest but not of the exact date because you had to stop me."

"I nearly stopped you sooner. You kept your voice down until the last sentence, which you repeated three times, very loudly and in French. The warder may have overheard."

He probably had, for he stared at me until we were safely in charge of one of his colleagues and had passed beyond the steel door which was locked behind us. We were herded into a Romanesque kitchen with so many chimneys that it looked like an impossibly complicated cruet. Had I been less abstracted I would have noticed that it was similar to the one at Glastonbury. A tourist bolder than the rest withdrew a few yards to take a photograph and was sternly ordered back to our pseudo chain-gang. On our way to the refectory we passed several barred gratings among the flagstones. Were convicts now suffering as had rebellious monks in underground punishment cells? These, as a contemporary records, were 'damp, lit only by a narrow barred window; the bed a stone slab covered with mouldy straw', in which 'on a diet of bread and water they soon became so blanched and skeletal that they seem like spectres rising from the tomb'.

"Pray for the soul of a German...." kept echoing in my brain, and did not cease its insistent beat until we came to the cloister where, in spite of the neglect of the garden they enclose, a fugitive peace lingers. I felt a lightening of spirit, a strong assurance that the prisoner had been set free of his ghost.

Then we came to the vast abbey church, where there is no altar, and the bone-bare walls have been ruthlessly stripped of their frescoed plaster revealing the stark stone. Here there is a sense of extreme emptiness, an awareness of the deliberate withdrawal of the Host.

It is a shock suddenly to see four great tombs in their solitary splendour: and even more startling to discover they are royal tombs of the great Plantagenets of England, the loom on which is woven the tapestry that is the historical background of the Lot. Here lie Henry II and his queen, Eleanor of Aquitaine. Beside them lies their son, Richard I, the Lion Hearted, and Queen Isabel, wife of his brother John, the King who gave us Magna Carta.

Henri II gave orders for his burial at Fontevrault shortly before he died, at Chinon in 1191. His affection for the place probably stemmed from the days when his aunt-by-marriage, Mathilda, became the second of a long line of abbesses, many of whom were of royal blood. Mathilda, a daughter-in-law of Henry I and granddaughter-in-law of William the Conqueror, admirably fulfilled the requirements of the abbey's charter, which decreed that the abbess 'should not be a girl who from early childhood had done nothing except sing psalms', but be, 'a woman of the world, capable of understanding and directing temporal affairs, and able to thwart the malign schemes of others'.

Although the founder of the Order, Robert d'Arbrissel, lived at a time when the two commandments of Jesus had not yet become so obscured by the ten Mosaic laws of the Jews, he must have been a great Christian to be able to found a community in which monks and nuns were not cut off from the opportunity of loving such of their neighbours as happened to be of the opposite sex. He took as his authority the words spoken by Christ from the Cross to His mother and John: *"Mére, voilá ton fils; fils, voilá ta mére,"* and told the monks to remember that the filial devotion which John gave to Mary should inspire them with similar fealty to their abbess.

There were some who grumbled that 'the omnipotence of women tends to create complications and difficulties'. But those with clearer perception recognized that the banquets and concerts, masques and fireworks, were far more pleasing to God than the sound of flesh tearing on racks or its stench from pyres which were being offered by contemporary theologians.

So it is fitting that Eleanor of Aquitaine should lie here; for, like the Magdalene who is the patron saint of the nuns of Fontevrault, her virtues were lucent, and her robust sins forgiven, because she had loved so much.

Chapter Four
ELEANOR OF AQUITAINE

Eleanor became Duchess of Aquitaine in 1137, when she was only fifteen. Her lands were almost as wide as those ruled by the dying Louis VI, so he sent the Dauphin hastening to Bordeaux to marry her; on their wedding journey he became Louis VII and she the Queen of France. She was wise, brave, gay and beautiful, but even at seventeen Louis was such an arid young man that his ministers had to order him to her bed.

In spite of his being, as she herself phrased it, 'More of a monk than a man,' she managed to present him with two daughters. But Louis did not want daughters, he wanted a son; and in the hope of persuading God to grant this boon, he made several pilgrimages to shrines within his realm, including one to the shrine of Roc Amadour, in the Lot. When this also proved fruitless, although they had been married for ten years, he reluctantly decided that God would not relent until he had been on a crusade. When he informed his queen of this decision she agreed that it was a wise one, and then dismayed him by pointing out that it would prove ineffective unless she came too.

He did his best to dissuade her, and so did his monks and ministers; but Eleanor stood firm. If she had to stay at home, then so would all the knights of her Duchy; knights who, as everyone knew, both out-shone and out-numbered those who owed their fealty only to the King. So, on the sound ethical principle that it is woman's duty to teach man to make love instead of war, and should she fail in this to share war's peril with him, the Queen and fifty of her ladies set off for the Holy Land.

It was an arduous and dangerous journey, on which

the women acquitted themselves admirably; and Eleanor, who, when an ambush was suspected, rode in the van with her knights, gained their even more fervent devotion by her unfailing endurance and courage. When at last they reached their destination she was delighted to find that conditions were far more congenial than she, or Louis, had anticipated.

Instead of ascetic warriors just managing to hold their own against the Saracen, she found that the knights who had remained there after the First Crusade—among them was her gay and devoted uncle, Raymond of Poitiers—had built themselves castles where they lived in far greater luxury than Louis had ever enjoyed at home. Not that Louis would have enjoyed luxury, for it is doubtful if he ever enjoyed anything except penances. In these, to the acute embarrassment of his hosts and their retainers, he frequently indulged, while they walked in close ranks on either side of him so as to conceal from the local inhabitants the undignified and unsettling spectacle of a king shuffling painfully to a shrine on his knees.

Had Eleanor always lived in her gay Duchy she would probably have been far too contented to play a vital part in history. But in the drab, narrow-minded Court of Paris, where she was constantly rebuked for her virtues by her masochistic husband, she stored up sufficient repressed energy for its release to result in the increased happiness of thousands of other men and women. Now, while Louis engaged in ineffective battles with the Infidel who continued to occupy Jerusalem, she was in the care of her indulgent uncle and free to think, and to act, and to be her real self. She learned how life for men as well as for woman could become an art, instead of an exercise in endurance, and she also acquired the materials for the background of this resurgence of living. Eagerly she accepted the comforts which had not yet penetrated to her part of Europe although they had been commonplace for centuries in the Middle East. Henceforward in her castles, and in the castles of those who owed her fealty, there would be carpets on the floors instead of rushes, arras on the walls, privies even for the men-at-arms. Women would dress to make themselves more beautiful; dress in silk, in velvet, in gauze, instead of bundling themselves in coarse wool to keep out the cold.

Although the Pope, whom they visited on their way home, had personally tucked them into a magnificently appointed bed erected for this express purpose in a room adjoining his oratory, she still failed to give Louis the son he craved, but instead did her best to put her new ideas into operation. The monkish Louis saw only one way out of this unbearable situation. He could not cope with his now rebellious wife so he must divorce her. And divorce her he did, in 1152; overriding the objections, both secular and religious, of his advisers with the pleas that 'although Aquitaine is desirable, an heir is essential to France'.

Lesser women would have been subdued by this indignity, but not Eleanor. For she had already fallen in love with a man of her own stature, Henry Plantagenet, Count of Anjou; and neither of them was in the least dismayed by the fact that he happened to be twelve years younger than herself. Two months after the divorce she married him, and within five months presented him with a son.

With a husband who not only loved but appreciated her, the ideas sown in Eleanor's fertile mind soon abundantly fruited. She set the fashions in which we still clothe the figures of the Arthurian legends and the romances of the Middle Ages; and when it became widely known that the Duchess permitted no man, however well-born, to enter her presence with 'his hair unkempt as a shock of barley', those who came seeking brides at her Court adopted clothes as decorative as the women's.

Under Eleanor's influence the arts flourished, espe-

cially the arts of music and poetry, and the troubadours she inspired sang her praises throughout Europe. Her Courts of Love were properly convened
Courts, presided over by Eleanor, and later by her
daughter, at which both boys and girls could seek
advice on their affairs of the heart, and where women
could gain redress against husbands or lovers. When a
man was found guilty of unethical behaviour, even if
this were only by being a boor, or a braggart, or a bully,
his punishment, which continued until he had made
full amends, was subtle but exceedingly effective. He
was completely ignored by the women. No woman
would speak with him, serve him, or even glance in his
direction, and if he were brazen enough to enter the
tilting yard the female spectators either withdrew or
turned their backs until his joust was over.

Eleanor, by her marriage to Henry, had added Anjou,
Maine and Touraine to the great possessions over
which they ruled. Within two years, these also included Normandy, for her husband, as Henry II, became Duke of Normandy when he succeeded to the
English throne. To do justice to the history of Eleanor
would take at least a quarter of a million words—four
times as many as there in this book, so I can here give
only a few highlights of her story.

By Henry she had five sons and three daughters. The
eldest, William, died in boyhood. The next, Henry,
nicknamed Courtmantle, of whom I shall say more
later, married her ex-husband's daughter, born of
Louis's second marriage. Geoffrey was made Count of
Anjou, and the two youngest, Richard and John, became Kings of England during her lifetime.

After twenty years of happy marriage with Henry, in
which she had only one enemy to marital peace, the
King's favourite, Thomas á Becket, they quarrelled so
bitterly that she left England and withdrew to her
Duchy, taking all her children with her except John,
whom she left with his father.

She loved all her children—but on Richard she lavished the devotion that Henry, under Becket's influence, had sorrowfully rejected. To make Richard independent she gave him her Duchy, which so infuriated Henry that he brought an army to France, intending to administer a sharp lesson in filial obedience. But Eleanor had been far-seeing enough to keep on good terms with her first husband's children; and Philip,

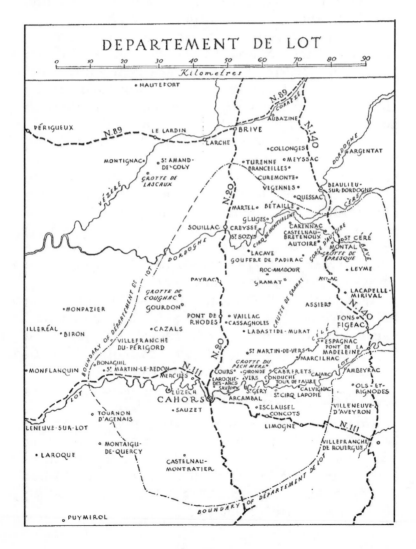

the son of Louis's old age, who had recently succeeded to the throne of France, sent troops to support Richard against his father.

Richard would have won even without this assistance, for most of his father's troops changed sides at the first battle. It would have been bitter enough for Henry if his troops had deserted through cowardice, but to see them turn against him on the field, ready to fight for their right to stay in what they already thought of as their own country, an English province in which the laws protecting the landless were so much more benign than the laws at home, was a blow to his pride from which Henry never recovered.

So it is primarily because of Eleanor that even to this day there are many families in the Lot who are proud of being descended from the English; who came not as conquerors but through rightful inheritance to govern beneficently for nearly three hundred years.

Chapter Five
FERDINAND DE LESSEPS

A pleasing alternative to following *routes nationales* through Blois to Brive is to take a more direct line by minor roads to join N. 20 between Argenton-sur-Creuse and Limoges. From the Indre to the Creuse there are many *étangs,* shallow, reedy lakes among flat pastures, where browse herds of cattle which look as though they were made of parchment coloured velvet, their ears and muzzles blushed with palest carnation pink. Here the wide placid vistas, the high skies, seem to belong to Holland rather than to France—a Holland of two hundred years ago, when the Low Countries could still offer to the painter's eye a landscape in water-colour virtually without figures.

But the quickest way from Chaumont to the Lot is via Blois and Chateauroux. When I came back from the Lot with Charles we went to Chateauroux, because we wanted to see the original of the portrait which is reproduced as the frontispiece of his biography of Ferdinand de Lesseps. We searched for it in several dreary galleries of the museum before at last discovering it tucked away in a little room above the stables—or what used to be stables when the château housed people as well as things. Below the portrait is the illuminated scroll which conferred on Ferdinand the Freedom of the City of London; and in dusty showcases lie the decorations showered upon him by seventeen countries after he had proved to them, in spite of their discouragement, that he could translate into reality his dream of linking the Mediterranean to the Red Sea by building the Suez Canal.

"You are the first people for a very long time to display any interest in the Comte de Lesseps," said the

44

guide sombrely, perhaps trying to excuse himself for the dustiness of the relics. After Charles tipped him he looked slightly more cheerful, but when we asked where we could find la Chesnaye, where Ferdinand usually lived when in France, he relapsed into gloom again at having to admit he had never heard of the place.

Had la Chesnaye not been obliterated by a worn fold of my map we could have reached it by turning east on to D. 34 five miles north of Levroux. But the only clues we had were references to the place in de Lessep's letters, which showed that although it was not far from Chateauroux the nearest town was Vatan. It was fortunate that we went there, for in the bar of the Hotel de France we met a Monsieur Merilhou, who not only knew the de Lesseps family but promised to conduct us to la Chesnaye after he had been home to lunch.

When he returned he brought with him a photograph of Ferdinand with his second wife, Hélène, and nine of their twelve children. He had also been kind enough to visit the stationers and ferret through a box of obsolete picture postcards until he found one of la Chesnaye. I was surprised that it looked as though it had been built early in the nineteenth century, for I knew that it had originally belonged to Agnes Sorel, the wise and beautiful mistress of Charles VII, whose tomb is in the château of Loches. One of her letters from la Chesnaye survives, in which she gives meticulous instructions for the care of her greyhound, Carpet, so named because he slept beside her bed and on chilly mornings used to warm her feet.

M. Merilhou had already told us that the de Lesseps family were no longer in residence, but I felt confident that so helpful a man would have managed to borrow the key. But when I hinted that it would be disappointing not to see the inside of the house, he said regretfully that we would not be able to see even the outside...for the place had recently been sold to housebreakers, who had pulled it down.

I was not entirely disappointed, for a biographer becomes closely identified with his subject and I was afraid that Charles might have found that an abandoned house evoked sad echoes of the old man, who lingered, deaf and senile, for two years after the tragic failure of the Panama Canal, rather than of the dynamic Ferdinand who had been so happy there with his first wife, Agathe.

As we got into the car, Charles was talking about Agathe, but I was again looking at the photography of Hélène. Even after bearing him twelve children she looked young enough to be his granddaughter, as she could have been, for when he married her she was only twenty and he sixty-four.

We took the road towards Guilly, and after three kilometres M. Marilhou told us to stop at what at first seemed to be farm buildings. But when we went into the great, square yard we saw that the stables which Ferdinand had built for his famous stud of horses were little changed, although now there were cows in the loose-boxes and grass was blurring the outlines of the paving stones.

Charles was saying, "The stud belonged to Ferdinand's mother-in-law, Madame Delamelle, who owned la Chesnaye. She, of course, was Agathe's mother...."

Why 'of course'? I found myself feeling illogically resentful. Why does no one bother to remember Hélène?

We crossed the road to look at a fine pair of iron gates which no longer lead into a château courtyard but only to an open space of tussocky grass that hides any trace of the foundations. In what had been the ornamental park there are still a few of the trees which Ferdinand planted. There had been many more, for they loved trees, but only stumps had been left by the timber merchant.

Charles was still talking in praise of Agathe..."It was his love for his first wife which gave him his extraordinary faith, his tenacity of purpose. If she had not died so young he might have been content to live quietly here, instead of turning his vast energies towards the creation of the Suez Canal...."

I wandered away from them, feeling unjustly impatient with Agathe. She had had her children by a young man who was ecstatically in love with her, and from one of them caught a lethal dose of Scarlet Fever. So she won posterity's admiration, by being adored by a famous man and dying young. But it was Hélène who had loved him when he most needed loving; Hélène who had remained unswerving in her loyalty when he was a failure, derided by the rest of the world. I came to a derelict conservatory, still clinging with struts of rusty iron to a garden wall. Had Hélène caused it to be built so that an old man could dream there, and forget that beyond the sheltering glass the winds of fame were blowing cold?

I heard Charles shouting to me that they were going to look at the chapel. Disconsolately I trailed in their wake across a field whose grass was flecked with the purple of autumn crocus. Had Hélène planted them here? It pleased me to think so, although I knew they grow wild in this part of France.

By the time I caught up with them they were already in the small nineteenth-century chapel. Cobwebs festooned the shabby altar, and a dusty rosary hung from a broken chair. Dead flies and fusty moths littered the sills of two grimy windows. Our kindly Frenchman was so embarrassed at the neglect that we did not linger there, and he was locking the door behind me when I saw Charles staring at an obelisk which until then we had not noticed because it was in the sombre shade of a great ilex.

It is a small obelisk, and on it is carved:

ICI
REPOSE LE SANG
DE
FERDINAND DE LESSEPS
Mort le 7 Decembre 1894
Embaumé le 9 Decembre 1894
SOUVENIR IMPERISSABLE!

Deeply moved, Charles began to read aloud: "Here lies the blood of Ferdinand de Lesseps...."

Perhaps if I had not remembered watching an embalmer at work in the Eleventh Dynasty of Egypt, I should not have realized the anguish of these words. Two days the body had waited for the embalmers to prepare it for its last journey to Paris, where it would lie beside Agathe's in the cemetery of Pére Lachaise.

But to Héléne, everything which had ever been part of Ferdinand was precious. So, when they had finished, she went alone into the bleak moonlight; to bury in the living earth all that remained to her of a great man's body: the strong bowels of his compassion and his brave blood.

A home at Collognes

Chateau d'Hautefort

Chapter Six
ROSE-RED VILLAGE

If Denys and I had followed N. 20 through Limoges, which although it is a large town takes only ten minutes, we should have reached Bive in under two hours, and found the scenery increasingly pleasing with every kilometre of that excellent road. However we made a long detour to Chalus, because I wanted to see the castle where Richard Coeur de Lion received his mortal wound.

He was laying siege to the place only because an antique gold statue had recently been unearthed in a nearby field, and the owner of the castle, believing it to have miraculous powers, refused to hand it over to his liege. Richard was enjoying a quiet evening stroll within bow-shot of the walls, no doubt believing that none of the defenders would be so foolhardy as to disturb the royal meditations, when a sentinel on one of the watch-towers could not resist so tempting a target and scored a gold in the King's shoulder.

The castle instantly surrendered. And Richard, who had seen many men die of sepsis after an arrowhead had been cut out, sent for his assailant: to congratulate him on his marksmanship and to grant him a full pardon. Regrettably, Eleanor, the Queen Mother, who reached Richard four days later only in time to watch him die, was too distraught to respect her son's clement wishes, and had the over-eager archer executed.

Contrary to my expectations, all that remains of the castle is part of a tower which is now in an unsalubrious farmyard. We had also been unlucky in my choice of a restaurant for lunch, so by the time we were descending the long hill to Brive I was wondering whether we might be equally disappointed with Collonges, where we intended to spend a couple of nights.

As I am used to Denys knowing my thoughts, I was not surprised when he said briskly, "You look tired and I'm hungry. Perhaps we should do better to spend the night here, to restore our energies before further exploring."

To give myself time to think, I pretended to be concentrating on the town plan in the *Guide Michelin* which was open on my lap. Had I romanticized Collonges when describing it to him? I had spent only a brief hour there four years ago, before the hotel was finished...and I had seen very little of the village because Charles was in a hurry and it was raining. But I had had a hunch that I should go back there, and be happy....

"We shall be in Collonges in about half an hour," I said encouragingly. "Cross the river—it's the Corréze, fork left at the market place and then look out for a sign on the left to Meyssac, D.38."

As wilting hydrangeas are revived by rain, so were we revived by the joy of that road to Collonges. There are more grandiose landscapes, but their skin of scenery is tightly stretched over the bones of form as though not a yard of the material of beauty could be wasted; but here it seems that there was so much beauty that it was prodigally used, the billowing embroidered silk allowed to fall lightly into its folds.

Within minutes of arriving at the Relais St. Jacques de Compostelle, we knew that our stay there would be longer than a couple of nights, and in fact we were cosseted by Monsieur and Madame Richier for five weeks. I had almost decided on a bedroom with a view of the medieval gateway and one of the little châteaux which, like the rest of the village, is built of stone the colour of dried rose-petals and has its towers capped with lavender slates, when Denys found that the rooms on the other side of the corridor look out to a vista even more enchanting—of curving fields and walnut orchards, that became our constant delight.

51

There are six bedrooms upstairs and two on the ground floor, and their simplicity, a bed, a table, two chairs, a built-in hanging cupboard, and a basin and bidet with really hot running water, was already a sign that we had found our favourite kind of hotel, experience having proved that an elaborate decor is too often associated with inferior cooking. On that first night we had *terrine maison,* several wafer-thin pancakes filled with mushrooms in a truffle sauce, a platter of delectable little trout, a salad and some goat's cheese. This is a very fair sample of the meals we thereafter enjoyed, although we were *en pension* and our bill, including tips, drinks, postcards, laundry and four prolonged trunk-calls to London, averaged thirty shillings a day each.

When we first saw them, the black coils of ancient vines showed only tentative tendrils, but by the end of the month they shaded the terrace from the noon heat and made a canopy of shade for the hen-roosts and rabbit-hutches. We saw the walnut trees, their gnarled branches mossed like the antlers of a stag in velvet, festooned with black chenille tassels that turned to bright cooper leaves, and then to heavy verdure studded with the glossy green of unripe nuts. The rich purple of catalpa and judas trees slowly waned as the scarlet cherries waxed, in such profusion that Denys seldom went for a walk without someone offering to fill his hat with them.

Our ears no longer had to act as sieves to protect us from the grind of traffic, constantly alert to let through only the essential information conveyed by voice, or car-hooter, or the telephone's insistence. Refreshed by the benison of silence, they could again bring us subtle news: the hot shimmering whirr of cicadas; the slow surge of wind in high grasses; the susurrus of poplars; the silver tuning-forks of gossiping frogs. And more robust but still genial noises: roosters ripping wide the curtains of the morning; the clash of saucepan lids; the measured tread of oxen; the creak of the winch which lifts them by a girth for shoeing, and their resonant bellowing when, freed from their yokes, they jostle to the drinking trough to suck water with a luscious squelching into their moist pink mouths.

And noses too came into their own. It was again instinctive to sniff an unfamiliar plant instead of only to look at its shape and feel its texture; to recognize that a field has quite a different smell at noon and at sunset; and to relish the sturdy smell of cow-dung in the strong old streets.

Unlike other twelfth-century villages of this region, with a castle poised for their protection on crest or cliff or crag, Collonges rests like a hare in her form among undular pastures. Here the nucleus is not a castle but a monastery, which had already been established for over three hundred years when, in 1077, Benedictines began building the present Romanesque church. The lovely tympanum over the west door is the keynote of this gentle place: a living Christ ascending on the up-surging joy of His attendant angels; while His mother and the eleven faithful apostles converse serenely on the love He hoped to teach them to remember.

Many were the pilgrims who rested here on their long journey to the shrine of St. Jacques de Compostelle, which is in the remote north-western corner of Spain. 'All roads lead to Compostelle,' might once have been an apt phrase, as is illustrated by the map at the Abbey of Conques, which I shall describe later. This pilgrimage played a significant role in England's history, for unless William X of Aquitaine had undertaken it, his daughter Eleanor would probably not have inherited his Duchy. Her mother, who had failed to conceive after the birth of a second daughter, Petronella, had recently died, so her father was at last free to marry and beget a legitimate son.

Being renowned for his amatory prowess, Duke William did not go to Compostelle to plead for heavenly assistance in this project, but as a penanance imposed on him by the Pope for quarrelling with that irascible ecclesiastic who later became canonized as St. Bernard. He travelled to Spain with a splendid retinue, and the day before arriving at their destination they encamped by a stream. In it were many fish, and although warned that these were held to be accursed, the Duke ignored the advice and ordered some to be prepared for his supper. He relished the meal, doubtless with a satisfaction akin to that enjoyed by the bold who introduce to gastronomy a fungus previously shunned by more timid mycologists. But during the night he was afflicted with a most grievous flux. However, although by the morning he was too weak to mount his horse, he insisted on being carried to the shrine on a litter. If he did so hoping for a miraculous surcease from his fleshly agonies he was not disappointed: for he expired in front of the High Altar at noon on Good Friday.

As Collonges is in a part of France too remote to have been much affected by the drab wave of parvenu mediocrity which polluted European taste in the nineteenth century, it suffered no change except by natural decay, shedding a stone here, a beam there, as trees shed their leaves in autumn. Many of the houses are no longer inhabited, for, in 1850, its prosperity finally waned when Meyssac supplanted it as capital of the Canton, and people drifted on the trade wind to the new centre which, although only two miles away, had a school and shops.

Collonges tried to fight back by acquiring a railway station, a little wooden building on the main road. But the engine was only strong enough to pull an empty carriage uphill, and one hopes that the vanished lines were beaten into ploughshares when novelty no longer tempted passengers to buy a ticket for the glide down to Turrenne, knowing that they would have to walk home.

A church on the Lot

Village marketplace

Now this lovely place is stirring to life again as it enjoys increasing fame through the devoted energies of Dr. Faiges, founder of the society of Les Amis de Collonges, who warmly befriended us.

His château of Vassinhac has been continuously inhabited since the fifteenth century, and during the Renaissance was embellished with carvings and tourelles. I do not know whether a local craftsman went to the French capital or a carver came from Paris to Collonges, but the Gothic doorway which opens directly to the wide spiral stair of the hexagonal tower is identical with the one in the Hôtel de Cluny.

The last of the Vassinhacs, who were Seigneurs of Collonges and governors of Turenne, to live in the château was Gédéon, and ardent Calvinist who aided Henri de Turenne, Duc de Bouillon, in a conspiracy against Henri IV. The conspiracy was discovered and Gédéon condemned to death, but he managed to escape and found refuge in Sedan. After a while the King, being a far more generous opponent than his late mother-in-law Catherine de Medici, granted him a full pardon with restoration of his lands and titles; so he was able to return home to a tranquil old age.

Turenne, as the crow flies, is only five miles from Collonges, but so lavishly is this landscape folded that roads are complex as veins in a vine leaf and there are eleven alternative approaches to the capital of the Vicomté, which once encompassed more than half the region now included in the *département* of the Lot. I think the best views are from the north, by D.8, for they caused Denys and me to get out of the car four times to photograph the town from a yet more pleasing angle. The narrow and precipitous streets should be explored on foot and at leisure, but a road coils up the conical hill, unfurling a panorama that can be seen in its entirety from the Tour de César. This, the earliest of the castle's defence works, is a single round tower with a spiral stair, narrow enough

56

to be held by one man and lit only by arrow-slots. After hearing Deny's enthusiasm for the view I regretted having been too lazy to follow him to the top, although I had enjoyed gossiping with a gardener who then took us to see the castle guard-room, the only part shown as the rest is inhabited.

For nine hundred years the Seigneurs of Turenne were independent rulers, owing neither allegiance nor tribute to the Kings of France. So the people flourished, until 1738, when their happy state declined because their Vicomte, to pay his debts, had to sell his feudal rights to Louis XV. That the majority of them feel the lack of a hereditary ruler, with whom to identify, and so nourish the most highly evolved elements in their own characters, was most poignantly demontrated in Brive on the 6th of May: when every radio and television in the town was the nucleus of silent people, listening intently and often moved to tears by Princess Margaret's wedding.

Chapter Seven
CLOSE TO COLLONGES

Before moving south into the Lot, I will mention some of the places which although outside the departmental boundary, are only about an hour's drive from Collonges, and begin with the most memorable, the Grotte de Lascaux.

Denys and I had spent most of the morning shopping in Brive when we decided that instead of going home to lunch we would prefer to spend the afternoon looking at prehistoric cave painting. So we left the town by N.89, and 11 kilometres later arrived at Les Glycines, in Larche. It was an excellent lunch, with the Vézère flowing past the dining-terrace, and the bill was only twenty-three shillings; so I asked Madame la Patronne to show me the bedrooms, which were futher evidence that it would be a delightful place at which to stay, especially as the full *pension* is only a guinea.

I had gossiped with her longer than I realized, so I was afraid that when we got to Lascaux we should be too late to be included in the three hundred and fifty people which, on my two previous visits, had been the quota allowed each day to enter the caves, because human breath was proving so much more destructive to the paintings than had the passing of twenty-five millennia. My anxiety proved groundless, for air-conditioning has removed this hazard and no longer do coach-loads of tourists arrive only to find that ten o'clock in the morning is already too late in the day.

Had I known this when we left Les Glycines we should have taken D.60 to Chavagnac and then a by-road through Chazel and Coly so as to see the fortified abbey church of St-Amand-de-Coly on our way. But instead we continued along N.89 and then turned south on N.704 to follow the Vézére to Montignac, a charming little town although crowded with tourists to Lascaux in the holiday season.

Prosperity came to Montignac through two trivial incidents: a tree was uprooted by a gale and a dog disobeyed its master's whistle. The tree tore a hole in the roof of a cave; but no one paid any attention to the hole except to cover it with branches to prevent cattle falling in, for there are more unexplored caves in this limestone country than there are bubbles in a litre of Perrier water. Then, in September 1940, a dog scrambled down the slope of fallen earth into the hole, and when it failed to reapppear four boys went down to search for it, taking resinous pine-knots with them to use a torches.

Two of these boys are now guides to the caves, and vividly convey the awed astonishment they felt when they first saw the treasure they had discovered, and the fear they felt also, for the animals seemed to be moving in the flickering torchlight, as they still seem to move, so instinct with life are they, even when one sees them illuminated by electricity.

One should go with humility to Lascaux, for anyone who expects to see paintings which, although interesting because of their extreme antiquity, are comparable only to those which might be expected from a talented child will receive a salutary readjustment of his historical perspective: and he would have to be remarkably obtuse not to recognize that the men who created these agile deer, these gay little ponies, this surge of mighty bulls, were not primitives to be patronized, but artists whose visionary insight was allied to the highest technical skill.

It was only half past four when we left Lascaux, so instead of turning right on N.89 for Brive we turned left, until N.704 took us northwards to Hautefort. This castle, with its massive domed towers and its double drawbridge across the inner moat, stands on a wide apron of formal gardens and dominates the surrounding landscape. It was altered and enlarged during the Renaissance, but the older part dates back another four hundred years, for it was originally owned by Bertrand de Born, knight and troubadour at the Court of Aquitaine.

After a temporary reverse in the arts of love, when Queen Eleanor's daughter Helen, to whom he addressed the most famous of his love-songs, was given in marriage to the Emperor Otto, he devoted his energies to the arts of war, by inciting Eleanor's eldest son to rebel against his father, Henry II. This was a remarkably foolish act, for the prince had recently been formally associated with the English throne and allowed to use the title of 'The Young King'—although still popularly referred to by his nickname 'Henry Courtmantle', and, even more important, he had just married the daughter and heiress of Louis VII, and so had every reason to look forward to inheriting the throne of both France and England. That he would never have done so, because Louis in his old age at last begot a son, Philip, by his third marriage, was a factor which Eleanor's fifteen years of marriage to Louis gave her no reason to anticipate.

Some historians suggest that Eleanor, and not Bertrand de Born, was the real instigator of the rebellion, but I feel sure she would have curbed her son's impatience until he had sired an heir; and most certainly she would never have permitted an act of such crass stupidity as the hot-headed young men committed when, either to replenish their war-chest with Church treasure or as a gesture of defiance against not only paternal but Papal authority, they pillaged the shrine of Roc Amadour.

The retribution for this sacrilege was immediate and ruthless. A priest of Roc Amadour cursed Courtmantle so effectively that he could retreat only to

Martel, a distance of fifteen miles, before he died; as a contemporary account records, 'lying on a bed of ashes, with a great crucifix heavy on his chest, in terror of certain damnation'.

Either Bertrand's capacity for human affection protected him from a similar malediction or else no black arrow was flighted in his direction, for all he personally suffered was grief for the death of his companion. But in fear of the royal rage he withdrew to Hautefort, where the King besieged him. Being far too experienced a soldier to prolong a siege when this could do no more than further exacerbate the besieger, Bertrand surrendered, and, as he expected, was condemned to death.

Bertrand the Warrior was within an hour of his execution when he was saved by the poetry of Bertrand the Troubadour. He claimed a boon, that Henry should allow him to sing the lament he had composed on the death of the young man they both so dearly loved. The boon was granted, and the King was so moved by the song that he pardoned the singer.

As Denys and I drove eastwards from Hautefort, I looked back to see it dark against a sky of funerary purple, a sombre mantling that might have been chosen for the place by Dante. For Dante, who could adore his Beatrice only if he did not have to test his capacity for loving in the crucible of living with her, set Bertrand in the Ninth Pit of the Eighth Circle of his Inferno, 'Carrying his severed head in his hand, lifting it by the hair as though it were a lantern, and sorrowfully declaiming, "Since you seek news of me, know that I am Bertrand de Born: he who gave ill counsel to the Young King, and made father and son rebel, the one against the other".'

This was harsh judgement on a fellow-poet, especially as Dante was usually mindful of the debt he owed to his forerunners the troubadours, and Bertrand became a monk before he died, so presumably received priestly as well as royal pardon. Or did Dante disbelieve in the sincerity of Bertrand's conversion, having identified him as the unfortunate whom six ladies of the Courts of Love emasculated after packing his loins in ice so that he should not cheat them of their justice by bleeding to death—a manœuvre which anticipated by eight hundred years the modern surgical technique of hypothermia. This stark punishment was supposed to have been inflicted on a gallant who boasted of his amatory success—a version which no doubt proved a salutary warning—but it seems far more likely that it was decreed by Eleanor when her innate chivalry was temporarily obscured by the anguish of bereaved maternity.

Each of the roads that cross the ridge to the northeast of Collonges has its individual merits. For instance, D.14 from Meyssac will eventually reach Aubazine, a hill village above the valley of the Corréze where there is a fine abbey church: but D.150, or alternatively D.10 and D.15, also leads there, through surprisingly different scenery. Often a side-turning from a lush valley winds up through richly variegated woods to reach abruptly a treeless upland of heather and broom and rocky outcrop; and to the east of N.140—one of the two great trunk roads which bisect the Lot from north to south—D.169 on its way to Argentat traverses an austere moorland, pine instead of walnut, bog-cotton instead of orchis. Yet other contrasts are to return from Argentat along the right bank of the Dordogne by the water's edge, or to keep south of the river and, by D.33 and D.41, follow the complex crests of forested ridges before the steep road winds down to Beaulieu-sur-Dordogne.

Denys and I went to Beaulieu several times, for it is only about half an hour from Collonges by the quickest route, D.38 and N.140, and was the nearest place where he could swim. I was surprised to find the water too low for him to use the diving platform which we found a few hundred yards upstream of the abbey, for in 1956 both the Lot and the Dordogne were flowing too fast for me really to enjoy bathing until July. But then they had been fed by the snowfalls of an exceptionally hard winter, and now we were seeing them after a mild one following a long summer drought. These rivers were not only affected by seasonal changes but also by the hydroelectric power stations in their upper reaches. When the reservoirs behind the dams are full the sluices are periodically opened to release the surplus, and so cause an abrupt increase in the current and volume of flow. It is to this phenomenon that the alarming riverside notices headed 'DANGER DE MORT!' refer. But although it would be foolish to camp on one of the islets, which appear only when the river is low, or below flood-level, which can easily be identified by flotsam caught on bushes, it is quite safe to swim unless the current is obviously running too swiftly. But swim upstream, for the banks are steep and slippery and it is only too easy to drift away from the place where you got into the water and then find it alarmingly difficult to find a firm foothold by which to get out again.

The eleventh-century Abbey of Beaulieu is renowned, especially for the tympanum of the south door, in which the contrasted environments of heaven and hell are further pointed by a frieze of vengeful and apocalyptic beasts. The town is also the birthplace of Baron de Marbot, whose vivid memoirs describe his rise to Lieutenant-General in Napoleon's army, but I doubt if many of the inhabitants who daily pass his statue are aware that this remarkable man was the prototype of Conan Doyle's 'Brigadier Gerard'.

The statue should be equestrian, for Marbot's beloved mare, Lisette, was as outstanding as her rider. He bought her for 1,000 francs, a fifth of her value, because she suffered from the bad habit of biting like a bulldog and had recently disembowelled her groom

63

with her teeth. For the next five months it took four or five men to saddle her, and they could only put on her bridle after covering her eyes and fastening all four of her legs. During this period she bit several people, including her owner, and he was thinking of selling her, albeit reluctantly for she was an incomparable ride, when a new groom, 'a man who was afraid of nothing, before going near Lisette whose bad character had been mentioned to him, armed himself with a good hot roast leg of mutton. When the animal flew at him to bite him, he held out the mutton; she seized it in her teeth, and burning her gums, palate and tongue, gave a scream, let the mutton drop and from the moment was perfectly submissive to him and did not venture to attack him again.' Marbot then tried the same tactics, whereafter Lisette 'became as docile as a dog and allowed me and my servant to approach her freely...but woe to strangers who passed near her!'

At the Battle of Eylau, Lisette richly rewarded her master's faith in her. Carrying Napoleon's order of retreat to a hopelessly outnumbered regiment, across a plain swarming with Cossacks, Lisette, 'lighter than a swallow and flying rather than running, devoured the intervening space, leaping the piles of dead men and horses, the ditches, the broken gun-carriages, the half extinguished bivouac fires'.

Their mission accomplished, Marbot was returning, carrying the eagle of the regiment, when he was temporarily paralysed by a glancing blow from a cannon ball on the nape of his neck, and so unable to defend himself against a bayonet attack by a Russian grenadier. The bayonet, deflected by Marbot's cloak, wounded Lisette in her thigh. 'Her ferocious instincts being restored by pain, she sprang at the Russian and, at one mouthful, tore off his nose, lips, eyebrows, and all the skin of his face, making him a living death's head, dripping with blood. Then, hurling herself with fury among the combatants, kicking and biting, Lisette upset everything she met on the road. The officer who made so many attempts to strike me tried to hold her by the bridle; she seized him by his belly and carrying him off with ease, she bore him out of the crush to the foot of the hillock, where, having torn out his entrails and mashed his body under her feet, she left him dying in the snow.' One is thankful to discover a few pages later that both Marbot and Lisette made a complete recovery, and for many more years enjoyed exploits together.

It is seldom that a château, or even an inconspicuous ruin, escapes the notice of Michelin's cartographers, but they have overlooked Curemonte—as we should have done but for the kindly advice of the owner of the Meyssac garage. Follow D.38 eastwards through Meyssac, then fork right on D.106 to Branceilles where, after a sharp left turn, the road winds through meadows until, beyond a crest, Curemonte and its village suddenly come into view. It seemed a scene unchanged since the Middle Ages, for if in fact it was flawed by a telegraph pole or patches of corrugate iron my memory has tactfully deleted them. The outer walls and towers of the castle are virtually intact, although within it is partially ruined and only a portico on the far side is occupied. Until recently it was owned by Colette's second husband, and although she visited it only briefly her daughter lived there for many years.

I have since been told by friends that Curemonte has a second château—a deserted one, which a villager suggested they might like to explore. They did so, and found it curiously eerie for it seemed to have been so abruptly abandoned, with cobwebbed but still sound furniture beyond the unlocked doors, and uncracked dishes on the kitchen shelves. When they asked to whom it belonged, the answer was always an evasive: "No one lives there." But I have not been to it; so for all I know the owners left only for some mundane reason, such as a sudden craving for an adequate water supply.

For the only water comes from two communal wells. I stared down one of them, trying to gauge how much effort it would need to draw up a bucket; the dark water was a long way down, for my reflection was no larger than a silver coin.

Curemonte lies at the northwest corner of a rectangle of byroads on higher ground, and by making this circuit it is seen from vantage points which are most rewarding. Even if in a hurry, at least go south from Curemonte to Vegennes—little more than a fine farm-house and a few cottages, turn left at the crossroads on to D.144, and pause on the ridge to look back at the little town spread out on its southern slopes like an embroidered apron.

The road soon forks, and both lead to D.153, at which turn right, and at the T road, D.12, right again to the hamlet of Queyssac. One eats well at the Au Vin Paillé—in the cool shade of plane trees if the day be hot, and is comfortable if one sleeps there. Queyssac not only provides a magnificent view of the Dordogne valley but is the home of the wine after which the hotel is named. This somewhat resembles Madeira, but is, uniquely, made from grapes allowed to ripen on the vine until they are about to fall from the stalks and then spread on straw mats—'paillé', on which they remain under shelter until pressed during the Twelve Days of Christmas.

From Queyssac, D.12 winds down to Bétaille, which, at last, is in the Départment du Lot. It is from this village that I made my first journey by Michelin, the little tram-like trains which, cooing like amorous pigeons, thread their way across the high plateaux and, often by tunnel or corniche, along the river gorges. Their lines cross and recross the roadways and at night the guardians of their gates are inclined to leave them closed, and can be aroused from sleep only by banging on the door of the adjacent cottage.

When I went to Bétaille to inquire at what time I should leave next day so as to reach Paris in time for dinner, the kind woman in charge of the miniature station become so engrossed in the details of this adventurous project that she failed to notice the approach of a train until it had bustled past the station uttering reproachful toots. Her reaction to this incident was so dramatic that I thought she was suffering from a heart attack. "The gates were not shut...not shut!!!" she cried, in tones of horror that would have been appropriate only had the level-crossing been strewn with the still-twitching corpses of passengers and mashed motorists.

Feeling guilty that my verbosity had numbed her natural alertness I administered what comfort I could, and eventually discovered that her emotion was caused by the knowledge that the driver of the Michelin, with whom she had a private feud, would undoubtedly sneak about her oversight to the stationmaster at Brive.

From Bétaille D.20, crossing the Dordogne, leads to a left turning on to D.30 for St. Céré, a friendly little town with several good hotels, overlooked by the Tours de St. Laurent, once owned by Eleanor of Aquitaine and now by Jean Lurcat, the well-known designer of modern tapestries. But Eleanor was a comparatively recent illustrious inhabitant of St. Céré, for the name derives from Espérie, daughter of a local landowner, Serenus, who, in the eighth century, caused it to become a place of pilgrimage. About the year 760 Serenus died, leaving properties whose ownership was disputed by a neighbouring seigneur, Ellidus. Seeking an amicable settlement, Espérie's brother betrothed her to Ellidus, but she, being a Christian and Ellidus refusing to join her faith, fled to the forest rather than submit to this expedient marriage. Her brother pursued her, and when she still refused to obey him he became so incensed that he drew his sword and decapitated her: at which, no whit disturbed, she picked up her head, carried it to a nearby spring and washed it.

Chapter Eight
QUATORZE JUILLET

When Charles and I spent a month at St. Céré we ate and slept at the Truite Dorée to the sound of rushing water; but when Denys and I went there, the Bave, a tributary of the Dordogue, was stagnant behind its weirs. The hotel was under new management and I was unable to introduce him either to Monsieur and Madame Gaboriau or the trout they used to gild with butter; so I will bypass these disappointments and go back to an earlier memory, the *Quatorze Juillet* 1956.

The weir by the Truite Dorée marks the western boundary of the water in which angling is permitted only for one *hour* in the year. Just as the red-deer of Scotland know the limits of their sanctuaries, so do the fish of St. Céré know theirs. There are no trout among them, for these have been driven away by their coarser brethren, carp and pike, who jostle for the swill cast from kitchen windows or tipped from buckets off a bridge.

Very fat do the fish grow, and only those who have also grown foolish drift over the weir, where anglers stand in wait with the patience of frontier guards. But on Bastille Day, the fourteenth of July, the fish of St. Céré have their placid routine rudely interrupted—and are probably as startled as were the five prisoners of the Bastille in 1789 when the crowd broke in.

Early in the morning the parapet of the road beside the fish-sanctuary, and the five bridges which span it, are divided by chalk marks into spaces, two metres wide and neatly numbered. To each space an angler is allotted, and, as some positions are far more favourable than others, these positions are decided by ballot.

By 2:30 p.m. about a hundred anglers had assembled in the Place de la République. So had the town band, various notables and officials, and a large number of spectators. I was surprised to see that several women and three children were competing; for at no other time did I see fisherwomen in the Lot. No doubt they considered the substantial money prizes, one for the largest and one for the smallest fish, made this event a worthwhile, instead of a time-wasting, occupation. Everyone seemed unusually solemn—probably because it was raining. The anglers formed themselves into a procession, and led by the band—now in full blast—marched through the town with rods at the slope.

After officials had made sure that the ticket pinned on each angler matched the number of the space in which he stood, the 'Off' was given by three shots from a revolver. Like a hundred-thonged flail the rods swished down, but, which seemed almost incredible, none of the lines became entangled.

Knowing how tame and greedy were the fish, I expected action. Minutes passed and nothing happened. The rain became heavier, until the drips bouncing on the surface must have caused all but the most feckless fish to shelter under the bridges. Spectators, looking rather guilty for deserting, began first to drift, then to scurry away. I was among them, glad that in France it is considered unmannerly if not actually insane, unnecessarily to defy the weather. But the anglers stayed at their posts, drenched but determined, until released at the end of their sixty minutes by a single revolver shot. Both prizes were won, so their fortitude must have been rewarded by at least two fish. But I did not see either of them, for by then my clothes were hanging up to dry and I was peacefully reading in a hot bath.

That evening, after the rain had stopped, I again found myself a spectator in the Place de la République, and this time a most reluctant one, for we were there to watch a troupe of funambulists. The high-wire for their act was strung between two masts, each topped by a flimsy crow's-nest, and glistened tautly above sixty feet of netless space.

When we arrived, the decision had just been made that the sodden ground would, after all, provide adequate purchase for the guy ropes of this dizzy edifice, and one of the troupe was anxiously trying to drive the pegs farther into the gravel.

I would have cravenly retreated, had not the proprietress of our favourite Café de la Paix pointed eagerly to the table she had reserved for us. Every table outside the Hôtel des Tourists and the other two cafés was already taken, so I had to pretend that nothing pleased me more than being ushered to a vantage point where I could not avoid seeing every detail of an accident, even if an unlucky acrobat did not actually land in my lap.

A gramophone was blaring through a loudspeaker on the top of a small green van. It broke off, and a voice announced that the death-defying performance of Mario Valesco and his troupe, which we were about to witness, would take place eighteen metres above the ground, without a net. 'Without a net!' was thrice repeated.

The first turn was not too alarming, for the blond young man, carrying a long flexible pole—the *balancier*—negotiated the wire without apparent difficulty; and when the crowd displayed not the slightest interest did it again rather faster. Applause still came from only about a dozen pairs of hands in the crowd who were standing six deep on the far side of the square.

I began to feel a little more cheerful, thinking that if this performance was as dangerous as it looked they would not be so apathetic. Their apparent apathy, in fact, was a studied rebuke to the Town Councillors who had made the unpopular decision that there should be a collection for the troops in Algeria instead of the usual *Quatorze Julliet* celebration—a dance with unlimited free wine.

70

The voice now announced that Mario, the world famous...the most daring...the greatest...funambulist would now appear in person.

Mario was a small man, with a thin brown face and a body as tough and flexible as juniper wood. He nodded to the crowd as though he did so only because it would be discourteous to ignore them. Using the *balancier* he did the double trip across the wire with elegance; then, after the voice had pointed out how difficult this was, crossed it again with only his outstretched arms to steady him.

Without bothering to acknowledge the spatter of applause, he slid down the rope and beckoned imperiously to one of the blond boys, who came forward carrying a heavily padded coat. After Mario had put this on, a rucksack was strapped on his back which held, like cartridges in a bandolier, a row of large rockets.

The voice now shouted that we were to have the inestimable privilege of being the first audience in the world to see a man become a *feu d' artifice* eighteen metres above the ground.

"The first and the last," muttered Charles succinctly, "for when they go off they'll blow him off the wire."

Under the weight of the rucksack, Mario climbed the rope ladder slowly, almost clumsily. The blond boy shinned up the rope and waved to the crowd whose interest was at last apparent. The lights were switched off. Twice the fuse was lit, only to fizzle out. The audience was now so quiet that I could hear the third match scratch on the box. Now the fuse was throwing up a spray of sparks. Suspense heightened as Mario stepped on to the wire, dark against the sky as a great hawk holding a straw in its talons. With his *balancier* wavering in a dangerously wide arc he moved slowly forward. With a hiss like a cobra the first rocket went off—then another—then three together. On he went, slowly, implacably. Jewels of fire wove a headdress for him, and showers of golden rain his wings, as though a son of Lucifer were crossing the abyss between hell and heaven.

71

"That is one of the most beautiful things I have ever seen," said Charles. "It lacked only the music of Stravinsky's Fire Bird."

With Mario safely back on the ground, I thought the suspense was over. The lights came on again. As Mario went towards the loudspeaker van I saw that he was limping. Suddenly I felt a stab of sciatica down my left leg, and knew that it was his pain I was feeling, and not merely a flare-up of my own.

The gramophone was now rendering the Ave Maria—the only alternative record to a march by a brass band. The melancholy theme broke off in mid-bar and the voice boomed: *"Attention! Mesdames et Messieurs!"* and declared that Mario had offered to cross the wire carrying any young lady from the audience on his back.

Being convinced that no one could be foolhardy enough to volunteer I was startled when a girl, wearing a white shirt and tight black trousers, ran into the circle of the arc-lights and threw kisses to the audience. A few of them clapped—but they were mostly children who were perched on the statue of a stern gentleman in a cocked hat. She skipped lightly to the rope ladder, but let it swing away from her when she started to climb.

"She is certainly not much of an acrobat," said Charles, "or is this incompetence only part of the act?"

Was her nervousness part of the act too? Surely she would not let him carry her if she knew he was lame with sciatica? Or had I imagined his sciatica when all he had really been suffering from was a stone in the shoe?

I watched intently as he climbed up after her, and knew he was driving himself to defy an unfamiliar enemy: acute and almost crippling pain. For a moment they stood together in the crow's nest, the girl pleading, Mario becoming at first increasing tense, then openly angry.

"Not a suitable moment for a row," commented Charles; and the crowd, sensing something was wrong, became more enthusiastic.

The girl was by now either so frightened or so clumsy

that she nearly throttled Mario when she tried to scramble on to his back; and sweat was streaming down their faces before he got her securely in position. By the time he at last began to inch forward along the wire, I was praying for them even harder than I had prayed for a matador being gored in the Barcelona bull ring. He kept fairly steady until he got more than halfway. Then his *balancier* started to flail the air. The crowd's indrawn breath sounded like waves sucking at shingle, as Mario regained his balance and gained the other crow's-nest in a tottering run.

Applause was loud but brief, for a display of fireworks had already started in the riverside gardens. In a moment the crowd was streaming on its way to watch them; and the square was empty, save for the forlorn funambulists. Something had to be done to cheer them, so by the time Charles had ordered champagne they were sitting around our café table. Conversation depended more on mime and intuition than on words, for Mario and the blond boy came from Catalonia, and the other two were Czechs.

While Mario, after a detailed exchange of symptoms and sympathy with me, listened to a more erudite exposition on sciatica by Charles, I talked with the girl. She was French, and spoke freely, having, I am still not quite sure why, understood me to say that I had recently retired from a circus in which I had had a lion-taming act. She was a native of Toulouse where she had been a member of the *corps de ballet;* had a charming illegitmate baby—sex and father unspecified—which was being looked after by her mother; was twenty-one years old, and considered that nothing at all interesting had happened in her life until the wonderful, stupendous event of meeting Mario, with whom she had fallen instantly, passionately and forever in love ten days ago. "So of course I had to join the act," she added, as though nothing could be more obvious.

She was deeply concerned about Mario's pain. "He is so *ashamed* of being in pain, and so *angry* when I talk about it. Because I talked about it so much and tried to stop him appearing tonight he thought I was accusing him of being afraid; which was why he insisted on working without a net. It is very frightening to work without a net." She sighed deeply. "All night he does not sleep: he groans: he twitches: it is torture to watch him." She lowered her voice. "So dreadful is his pain that for the last three days he cannot even make love! Have you perhaps some medicine...?"

I was not sure whether she meant an anodyne or an aphrodisiac, but having a supply of the first commodity I was about to fetch some from the hotel when Charles guessed my intention and said: "Mario has just told me that he has been getting injections of morphia from various quacks. I have told him that tomorrow he must see a proper medical practitioner. It is far too serious for optimistic amateurs to handle."

I knew that the last remark was a firm hint to me, so I could do nothing more helpful than arrange to meet them the next morning, and help them find a doctor.

For this assignation I dressed with some care, feeling that the medical profession would be more likely to take trouble about my protégés if I assumed the role of English country gentlewoman, rather than that of an out-of-work performer with the great cats. But I had forgotten that this was a French Sunday. I went to the home of every doctor in the town, and all of them were taking Sunday off. I visited St. Céré's splendid dentist, Monsieur Pirot, who had made Charles an excellent gold tooth, but he too had gone away for the day. I rang up two thermal establishments which treated rheumatism, and so might have taken interest in a sufferer from sciatica, but without any useful result.

Subdued, I went to report my failure. Mario was sitting on a hamper with his head in his hands. Before I could speak to him I was intercepted by an old lady in black who last night had been taking round the collecting box. She introduced herself as Mario's mother, apologized bleakly for her son's ill manners which had prevented him inviting her to join my party—and then launched into a tirade against the girl who had bewitched him at Toulouse; the girl who was entirely responsible for his sciatica, the girl who had thrust herself upon his family, and who was so arrogant that she thought that with a snap of the fingers she could become worthy of a world-famous—*the* world-famous—funambulist, and could make him disobey his mother and refuse to enter hospital!

At last she had to pause for breath and I had a chance to say that it was natural and healthy for sons to disobey their mothers: that many English mothers also found it painful when their sons grew up, but...

She interrupted: "Madame, we Catalonians are wiser than you are. We know how to protect our sons." Her eyes were as obscenely wise as the eyes of an ancient tortoise. "Early this morning I telephoned to Toulouse to engage the services of a funambulist who is only a little less famous than is my Mario. He demanded a disgracefully high salary—but I have my private savings. Mario will have to agree to go into hospital now that the act can continue without him. The girl says she will visit him daily—but as you will soon see for yourself, Madame, the girl will stay with the act, and give my son time to forget she ever existed."

"But why should she leave him?" I said indignantly.

The tortoise lifted her wrinkled eyelids to loose at me a stare of profound disdain. "Look behind you, and learn the wisdom of a mother."

Reluctantly I obeyed. Getting out of a car was a magnificent hunk of man. The girl was gazing at him as he pulled off his shirt and luxuriantly flexed his muscles; gazing at the bronzed shoulders on which, above cheering crowds, she would safely ride.

She glanced at Mario, and I heard her say: "My darling, I insist that you go today into hospital. Your mother and I together will look after the act."

A dovecot (above)
Aux Bonnes Choses (below)

Chapter Nine

CHATEAU AND CHATELAINE

The rose-red castle of Castelnau-Bretenoux crowns a great crag which rears up from the placid fields of the Dordogne valley, seven kilometres from St. Céré. Its keep was built before William of Normandy conquered England, and by the Hundred Years War it had become a mighty fortress. The massive, towered walls are footed by a deep ditch, which must further have discouraged enemies who had managed to reach it before being shot down by the castle bowmen. It seems unlikely that even when a strong force marched against them the occupants felt much anxiety, for the enemy had to advance across open ground with only impregnable stone walls as a target for their archers, whilst the home side, ensconced on the height above, could pick them off at leisure; an easier and less dangerous quarry than the wild boars and wolves they were accustomed to hunt in the neighbouring forests. If a few arrows were flighted high enough to cross the outer walls it would be a very lucky shot that did more than clatter harmlessly into the courtyard, perhaps startling a horse—of which two hundred were stabled within the precincts.

The family of Castelnau de Bretenoux flourished until 1715 when the dynasty ended through lack of an heir. The castle was sold and resold both before and after the Revolution, and in 1851 the owner attempted to get rid of this huge white—or rather, rose-red—elephant by insuring it for the equivalent of £1,000 and then trying to destroy it with fire. Fortunately he only partially succeeded, and was so inefficient that the insurance company contested the claim, which resulted in his being gaoled for attempted fraud; and in gaol he died.

Soon afterwards, a woman of St. Cirq-Lapopie had her fourteenth child, a son who was christened Jean. When her husband died, neighbours adopted several of the children; for she could take only the four youngest with her when she went as *femme de ménage* to a nearby farm, it being understood that they would earn their keep by working for the farmer when they were old enough. Three of them did so, but Jean always neglected his chores and wandered off, singing. By the time he was eight they gave up scolding him and let him look after the goats.

He was singing while his goats nibbled at the verges, when along the road strolled an opera singer from Paris, who was so entranced by the quality of the boy's voice that he not only paid for his musical education but adopted him.

The little goatherd sang his way to fame, and became Monsieur Jean Mouliérat of the Opera Comique who, in 1896, purchased Castelnau-Bretenoux. His mother had by then been dead for many years, but the farmer who had befriended him as a child was still alive; and because he had always wanted to own a vineyard, vines were planted for him at the castle so that he could enjoy them in the quiet evening of his days.

For thirty-eight years Jean Mouliérat divided his genius and his gusto between becoming an even more famous tenor and restoring Castelnau-Bretenoux to much of its former splendour. He wisely did not attempt to rebuild the part of it that had become a picturesque ruin, but there were many rooms untouched by fire, and these he indefatigably traced the original furniture which had been sold half a century before to pay the debts of the unlucky arsonist. The habit of collecting must have grown on him, for the rooms are overcrowded—unless perhaps some of the furniture was brought here from his home in Paris after his death.

A few days before he died, in 1932, he gave the castle and its contents to the State, with a proviso that photographs of himself in his favourite operatic roles should be displayed therein—they look incongruously old fashioned—and that the two little rooms where his great friend Pierre Loti wrote several books should not be shown to the public until after the death of his, Jean's, last surviving relative who might wish to use them.

Presumably she was still alive when Charles and I went there, for they were not officially on view although the guide let us see them when we told her that I was writing a book about the Lot. After the usual conducted tour, in which we were the only participants—for it was a weekday in June—she gave me a sprig of orange blossom from one of the trees growing in tubs on the rampart garden and tactfully suggested that we might like to wander round alone while she waited for us at the gate-house.

After lingering in the warm sunshine to enjoy the view, which would have been even more impressive had we bothered to climb one of the towers, we went back to the oratory. Here there is a magnificent triptych whose quality had been recognized only the year before when someone from the Beaux Arts sent it to Paris to be freed from the layers of dirt, no doubt augmented by smoke from the arsonist's fire, that had allowed it to remain undisturbed when the rest of the contents was sold in the nineteenth century.

A full length portrait of St. Bartholomew as a young man is surrounded by fifteen smaller, vividly detailed pictures depicting his life and martyrdom. Yet even the one which shows him being flayed is not horrific, for he smiles so benignly that at first I did not realize why his face was as pink and smooth as a baby's, or why it lacked hair and eyebrows. The executioners who are stripping his skin from the living flesh might be valets removing his clothes, and the mask, with its long white beard with hands upside down between his knees, be no more than a disguise he had put on for a fête on a summer evening.

79

As I looked again at the young Bartholomew I saw that what I had first thought to be a black dog, patient on its haunches beside him, is not a dog but a small demon. The demon's horns are pricked like the ears of an attentive hound: it wears a collar and is led by its master on a leash of gold links, a symbol of mutual affection. For Bartholomew was no longer afraid of his demon, no longer trying to starve or scourge it into submission. Instead he had accepted the responsibility of training it by compassion to work with him in their Master's service, as a good shepherd works in charity with his dog.

In the oratory of St. Bartholomew, on 30th October, 1475, Antoinette de Castelnau de Bretenoux married her father's companion-in-arms, Robert de Balsac. It is a little surprising that he chose her instead of an Italian bride, for he had spent most of his adult life at the courts of Florence and Milan and found their culture infinitely more congenial than that of France. He may have married her only because she was beautiful and then found she was unbearably dull, or else she was too timid to face foreign travel, for when he returned to Tuscany, as governor of Pisa, she stayed with her parents, and only saw her husband when he returned for brief visits, during which he provided her with five children.

One of these, his eldest daughter Jehanne, he deeply loved; and frequently promised her that one day he would come home to build a château which would surpass any he had seen in Italy. When Jehanne married Almeric de Montal—who was governor of the Haute-Auvergne, her father's natal province—she considered it her duty to stay near her mother, and so lived in the castle, within sight of the ancestral walls of Castelnau-Bretenoux, which had been given to her as a dowry. Here, only a mile to the west of St. Céré, she lived for the rest of her long life, and, like her mother, had five children, two of whom died in infancy.

She had been married for six years when in 1503 her beloved father at last came home, but only to die: and in 1511 Jehanne became a widow. Now she had no one to divert some of the consuming devotion she had always felt for her eldest son, named Robert after her father, who became the focus of her passionate emotional life. He was already showing signs of having inherited her grandfather's wanderlust, and so Jehanne, being too intelligent to try to curb him by less subtle means, decided to create, within the outer walls of her castle, such a glorious Renaissance château that he would be forever content to stay at home.

Nothing must stand in the way of realizing this dream, and she launched herself upon the task as though trying to woo a cooling lover from a rival mistress. She even wrote to the King for his advice, and François Premier, no doubt touched by this maternal temerity, allowed her to employ his finest craftsmen.

A foundation stone gives the date when the work began:

'Jehanne de Balsac, Dame de Montal,
Cette œuvre fit edifier l'an MCCCCCXIII'

It was not enough that the staircase be incomparable; the underside of each tread must also be carved, and carved in a manner worthy of the splendid chimney-pieces and the ceilings of the serenely proportioned rooms. Robert should have cultured youths instead of uncouth men-at-arms to serve him: so the *salle des gardes* is a setting for courtiers, with a walnut dining-table six metres long which still gleams like peat water, and an inside stair to the kitchens so that the food which might help to keep Robert's friends contented in this quiet country district should be served piping hot.

When she woke in the great bed under its baldaquin—whose yellow silk-damask is neither faded nor frayed although it is more than four centuries since it was loomed in Lyon—she must often have heard the clink of chisel on stone as a carver worked on the entablature of a window, or the lintel of a doorway, or added a detail to a frieze.

For twelve years the Château de Montal grew slowly towards perfection; and then, as though a spell had been cast upon it, all work ceased: except to add to the *lucarne* of a window the headless figure of Robert, with the anguished device 'PLUS D'ESPOIR'. For Robert had been decapitated at the Battle of Pavia.

In the torment of bereavement Jehanne refused to be comforted by the fact that she had a younger son, Dordé, who had entered the Church. She must even have looked on him as the usurper of Robert's inheritance, for when the Pope decreed that Dordé be released from his vows she replied indignantly that she would infinitely prefer the line to die out. But her wishes were overruled, so that Montal should remain in the hands of a powerful Catholic family, and Dordé reluctantly gave up the austerities of his monastic life to live under the more rigid discipline of his mother.

The Pope demanded an heir, and so an heir must be provided. Dordé was given no choice in the matter, for Jehanne selected as a daughter-in-law her niece, Catherine de Castelnau. Jehanne's daughter, Anne, also lived at home, although she was married, but the Dame de Montal never relinquished a moiety of her authority and had outlived them all when, as a very old and lonely woman, she at last died.

Was it Jehanne or Robert who returned to rescue Montal during the early years of the present century? If it were neither, why did a petroleum millionaire, Maurice Fenaille, immediately decide, on seeing the stripped and desolate shell, that he would devote his energies and fortune to restoring the château to its former glory?

Montal, some thirty years earlier, had been brought by

a speculator who had sold not only the furniture but all the carved stonework, except the staircase—which fortunately proved too difficult to move—some of it passing into private hands although the majority went to museums in England, America and Germany. Maurice Fenaille indefatigably traced each item and bought it back, often after considerable opposition from museum curators. But the longest wrangle was over a chimney-piece which he eventually traced to the house of one of his cousins, for, as my informant wryly remarked, "No one ever drives so hard a bargain and still remains quite so disagreeable as one's own relations."

Each stone was fitted meticulously back into the space from which it had been ravaged, the work being so well done that it is difficult to believe that this lovely château was ever in need of restoration.

When Maurice Fenaille died, in 1937, he left Montal to the State. His eldest daughter, the Comtesse de Bily, still lives there; and the portrait busts of Jehanne, and her father, and her husband, and her two sons, and her daughter, and her son-in-law, look down at the courtyard and the east wing which she was too sorrowful to finish.

Chapter Ten
OF FEAR AND FIDELITY

The road up the Cirque d'Autoire turns south from
D.30 about a mile to the west of the Château de Montal.
Autoire is a beautiful village and its manor house looks
down at its reflection in an ornamental lake set in
weeping willows. Beyond the lake, vineyards slope up
to the rock-face which becomes increasingly precipitous until it reaches the crest of the gorge, where a
stream cascades over a sheer drop and becomes a
plentiful source of *écrevisses*.

Charles and I have enjoyed many of these freshwater
crayfish—although I have never succeeded in catching
any, for we went to the Manoire d'Autoire nearly every
day while we were at St. Céré, because our host, Jacques
de Colomb, thought I would be more likely to write
industriously there than in our hotel bedroom. However, it was Charles who worked on his manuscript and
I spent most of my time gossiping with the family.

Before knowing the Colombs I thought my instinctive gesture of so often shaking hands might be redundant even in France. But I soon learned that this fear
was groundless, and that to shake hands with everyone when I first saw them in the morning and again
before I left the house was by no means enough.
Courtesy demanded that everyone shook hands with
everyone else both before and after luncheon, even if
two of the participants had been chatting to each other
ten minutes earlier in another room, and was the
prelim and colophon of each subsequent encounter.
My record score was eleven hand-shakes with the same
person between meeting them at ten in the morning
and leaving the house at half past four.

But until the Colombs came to dine with us at the Truite Dorée I had not seen this pleasing custom in full flower. The proprietors, Monsieur and Madame Gaborieau, met Monsieur le Marquis and Madame la Marquise at the doorway of their hotel; and shook hands. Madame Gaborieau's parents, Monsieur and Madame Landau, then came forward; and shook hands. The Gaborieaus were by now stationed at the door of the dining-room, and as we entered we shook their hands. After dinner, the chef, who was of course requested to accept fulsome congratulations, shook hands all round both before and after he had drunk with us a *digestif.* There was another round of hand-shaking when the Gaborieaus came to inquire whether we had enjoyed our meal, another with the same partners at the dining-room door, another outside the hotel—and a final one through the open window of the car.

Jacques de Colomb's mother had her eightieth birthday the day after we first went to Autoire. She was too crippled by arthritis to walk downstairs, but sitting in a high-backed chair in her bedroom, her hair vividly white under the ivory lace of her scarf and her eyes brighter than the antique diamonds on her fragile hands, she was gay as a young girl.

"I do not believe in phantoms," said Jacques as he introduced us to her, "but you will find that my mother shares many of your ideas, for she too has her visions."

"Had I not believed in my visions, as Jacques calls them, he would not have been born. So while he gives us our coffee I shall allow myself the pleasure of telling you the story—and hope that my son, who has often heard it before, will have the forbearance not to interrupt me."

After telling Jacques to move my chair closer to her, pleading a slight deafness which was only an excuse for asking me to repeat a remark when my French was more incomprehensible than usual, she began.

"I was sixteen when I dreamed a dream which

changed the course of my life. In the dream I found myself standing at my bedroom window, knowing I waited for someone, although I did not yet know who he would be or why he came. In the bright moonlight I saw a man walking towards me across the lawn. I could see his face very clearly and knew he was either very ill or in great pain. He stood looking up at me and then cried out in a voice of anguish: 'You must wait for me! I cannot come to you yet, but you must promise to wait for me!'

"My heart went out to him, but I could neither move nor speak. Then he turned and went slowly into the shadow of the dark trees. But as I watched him go I saw that he was wearng the tropical uniform of an army officer, and that his left leg had been amputated above the knee....In my dream it did not seem incongruous that in spite of this mutilation he walked without a limp.

"When I woke, the dream was still so vivid that it emboldened me to inform my parents that they must break off the plans they were making for my betrothal. They were displeased, for they considered their choice for me would be a most suitable alliance, and when I told them that nothing would make me break my promise to the man I intended to marry, they became incensed. It was difficult to convince them I had not been indulging in furtive assignations, but at last I managed to satisfy them that I had met my lover only in a dream...at which my mother was relieved and my father became even more angry, seeing himself as the victim of a daughter's hysterical whim.

"Looking back over the years I can sympathize with their anxieties, but at the time I thought them utterly heartless. I defended myself from their arguments with tears and tantrums, and when these failed, took to my bed and refused to eat. As in those days it was quite fashionable for girls to retreat into a decline when crossed in love, they eventually became sufficiently alarmed to summon the family doctor. He at least had the wit to realize that my malaise was not due to tight lacing, but suspecting an affliction of the lungs he advised the current remedy—a change of air.

"This verdict would gain me a respite, if no more, so I coughed convincingly until I was sent off to a friend of my mother's who had a daughter of my own age. You can imagine my feelings when in this girl's bedroom I saw a photograph of the man of my dream! To my overwhelming relief she told me that the photograph was not of her fiancé, as I had feared, but of her brother. I was, of course, not in the least surprised to hear that his regiment was in Indo-China, for his uniform had shown me that he was in a hot climate. But why were his family unconcerned by the loss of his leg? It was not until the following morning that I summoned the courage to ask such a pertinent question, and his sister was bewildered as they had not received news that he had even been wounded.

"Three days later the letter arrived containing the confirmation for which I had been waiting. When he was wounded he had refused to allow his family to be informed, hoping to spare them needless anxiety. Then the wound became gangrenous, and when the doctor told him that the leg must be amputated he thought the battlefield on which he would die would be the operating table. But he did not die, for, although he did not tell anyone about this until much later, just before the orderlies came to put him on the stretcher he saw a girl standing beside his bed; a girl who said he must get well because he had promised to marry her.

"Jacques' father kept his promise, but before so doing he kept me in suspense for nearly two years, by refusing to see anyone except his family. How many letters I wrote to his sister before I was at last invited to visit them again! How I tormented myself with fears that he might marry someone else! But at last we met, and he told me that it was a vision of me which had

87

prevented him from dying; but he had argued himself out of the belief that I was just a girl who was waiting for him to come home and marry her, and decided instead he had seen an angel sent by his mother's prayers to tell him that it was his duty to go on living."

Jacques, perhaps because he wished to conceal that he was moved by her story, said rather brusquely, "I shall believe in phantoms when I see one. But I am prepared to admit that odd things happen and that there are houses which I should prefer not to own. It is now my mother's turn to listen while I tell you about such a house, in which one of my cousins had to live after she married a Hungarian. He bred horses there and sired fourteen children.

"It was quite a modern house, built about 1790, and inconvenient even for Hungary, with two wings, one occupied by the parents and the other by the hordes of children, joined only by a ballroom and orangery—disused since the family fortunes declined after the Kaiser's war. My cousin might at least have been spared the knowledge that the place was haunted had she not decided to engage an English governess. They already had two governesses, a Frenchwoman and a German, who were so jealous when they heard that another one was coming that, to give the English girl some privacy, she was allotted a small suite above the orangery. These rooms had not been used for many years, but they were refurbished, and on the evening she arrived she seemed to be delighted with them. The footman who carried the dinner tray up to her sitting-room mentioned that she appeared to be very cheerful and had an excellent appetite, and that she intended to finish her unpacking before she went to bed."

Jacques paused to make sure he had our full attention. "But the poor girl did not go to bed. When the footman took up her breakfast tray he found her still fully dressed in the sitting-room—but she was dead. On her face was an expression of such terror that the doctor who did the post-mortem could only conclude that she had died of fright.

"This unfortunate incident was glossed over by calling it a heart attack, and so that the servants should not start rumours about the house being haunted it was decided that the next governess should have the same rooms. Perhaps my cousin did not fully share her husband's robust attitude, for she engaged a middle-aged Swiss to teach her children English: and when this woman arrived was relieved to find that she not only had an excellent English accent but was even more phlegmatic than her references and photographs had suggested. In fact, in a letter written to me that evening she called the new governess the 'Prussian Grenadier', and said it was a comfort to know that such a woman could not possibly be affected by phantoms for she was too stolid even to notice when the children giggled as she stroked her bristly moustache.

"However, a letter written three days later proved my cousin to have been unduly sanguine. This woman was also found, in the sittting-room, having not gone to bed. She was alive, but raving mad. So far as I know she is still in the Swiss asylum where she was eventually placed at the request of her family. My cousin bought them an annuity to cover the fees."

Jacques took off his glasses and polished them carefully before continuing. "These two unfortunate incidents were enough to cause the rooms to remain locked for three years...Hungarians tend to be superstitious. Then, although her husband disliked any mention of the subject, my cousin could not resist bringing it up when the conversation at a dinner-party turned to the supernatural. Among the guests were two young officers who had been friends since childhood. Staunch sceptics, they demanded to be allowed to spend the night in the haunted room. And their host, perhaps through fear of being laughed at, gave his permission.

"The ordeal started gaily enough. Servants were sent

to light the fire in both rooms and to make sure there was an ample supply of candles. Tokay, thermos flasks of black coffee, and a cold collation were provided for the vigil. Neither of the young men seemed in the least nervous, although one of them took his pistol with him, declaring that he would fire it at anyone who was foolish enough to try to scare them by masquerading as a ghost. By the morning they were both dead. But they had not died of fright: one of them had shot the other through the head, and then killed himself by firing a bullet into his own mouth."

Before I could say anything, Jacques gestured to me not to disturb his mother who had fallen asleep. "When she knows the story my voice does not keep her awake," he said wistfully as he held open the door. Then, more briskly, after he had carefully shut it behind us, "The third unfortunate episode caused my cousin to insist on having the rooms demolished. As events have turned, this was a pity, for the place is now occupied by communists, and the phantom could have played splendid jokes on a Russian general or a commissar!"

Chapter Eleven
BOOKS OF THE BLACK ART

A few days later, a thunderstorm, which had broken higher up the Dordogne valley and cut off the electricity supply, arrived at Autoire at three o'clock in the afternoon. Rain was driving horizontally across the precipice above the steep vineyard, and clouds the grey-purple of opium poppies pressed down on the gorge until it was too dark even to address white envelopes in black ink. So I left Charles determinedly touch-typing, and wandered disconsolately downstairs to the veranda where I found Jacques, who I saw had also been trying to work, for a pot of congealing glue stood on the flagstones beside a Louis Quinze chair.

"It is not light enough to see what I'm doing, and anyway, there is less and less money to be made from antiques," he said gloomily. "If only you had come here five years ago it would not be necessary to restore furniture, for we could have made a fortune from the treasure."

"But I thought the treasure your family buried here before the Revolution had never been found."

"Nor has it been...and you have not been able even to suggest where we should search." He sounded as though I were a child who had snubbed the grown-ups by refusing to join in a game of hunt-the-thimble.

"Then how could I have helped if I had come here earlier?"

"My mother assures me that you know how to deal with phantoms. Therefore you would have been able to decontaminate certain valuable objects to which is attached a curse."

"It depends on the curse," I said warily. "There are

91

objects, even in museums, with which I would not dream of meddling."

"But books? Surely you would not be afraid of six superb thirteenth-century books?"

"What kind of books?"

"The Black Art—and the man who wrote them seems to have been a most competent magician."

Only too appropriately, his remark was followed by a tremendous thunder-clap, and a gust which sent the curtain of creepers swaying like an arras in a draughty banqueting-hall. Jacques picked up the glue, found it was too cold to use, and decided that his time would be better employed in telling me a story. "You can put it in your book if you like, but change the names of the people involved and be sure not to reveal where the treasure was found...I'm always meaning to go and have a look there."

To this I of course agreed, and he continued, "The château where the books were found is in the Lot, but a long way from here, and was built in the twelfth century. The family became increasingly powerful until the Renaissance, then gradually became impoverished until the last one died when my mother was still a child...she remembers him as a very old man telling her that one day he would be rich again because he would have found the family treasure. But he died virtually a pauper and the place fell into ruin.

"Five years ago, a boy from the village went there to look for owl's eggs. The nest was on a ledge, which had once been the hearthstone of an upper room. Climbing up to it he dislodged some plaster which revealed a cupboard built into the thickness of the wall. The lock and hinges were still intact, but he managed to force it open and saw a large parcel of waxed linen, sealed with the same device that he had seen carved in stone in various parts of the château. Being too impatient, and too ignorant, to realize that the six layers of wrappings and the six great seals of purple wax should have been carefully preserved, he tore it open. He expected the treasure to consist of gold and jewels, and so was keenly disappointed only to find six large and very heavy books. However, he at least had the sense to leave them there and to hurry back to tell the mayor about them.

"The mayor, although having no conception of their actual value, realized the books were very old and so might fetch a good price for the benefit of the commune. So he wrote to a friend—whom you could call Desnos, who was by profession an archivist. Desnos was not particularly interested, for he thought they would be either muniments or household account books, of which he already had too many in the departmental archives; but being a conscientious man he drove to the mayor's house on the following Sunday.

"After luncheon Desnos did not allow the mayor to accompany him to the château, perhaps because he thought his host doubted his ability to find the cupboard unaided...Desnos was abnormally sensitive about having to wear such thick-lensed eye-glasses. Thunder was in the air, but he reached the château before the rain began although it started to fall heavily as he was mounting the staircase. The floors of some of the rooms into which he peered showed signs of rot, and he was relieved to find that the floor-tiles of the one he sought appeared perfectly sound. It was a small room and ivy had grown across the window, but he could see the cupboard, and by standing on tiptoe soon had the first book safely in his hands. A glance at it was enough to make his heart pound with excitement. Undoubtedly it belonged to the Middle Ages! And his hands trembled as he turned the pages, for he was looking at authentic records of the Black Art!

"He was too absorbed to notice certain ominous creaks and rumblings—or if he heard them he thought them no more than echoes from the thunderstorm. As he stretched up to reach the second book—would it too be bound not in vellum but in human skin?—with a great crash the floor gave way beneath him. He fell, but not far, for he found himself wedged between two joists which supported him under the arm-pits. He tried to struggle free, but when he moved so did the joists, and when the dust cleared he saw that his supports had been gnawed by rats and were tilting dangerously on the edge of their sockets. He decided that when he got his breath back he would let himself fall into the lower room, for it would not be too far as below him there must be a convenient pile of rubble. By craning his neck he could just get his glasses close enough to his hands to wipe them with his finger...and saw that he was suspended above the castle well, a sheer drop of eighty feet into black water.

"He shouted for help, although he knew that no one could hear him against the thunder. But he went on shouting: and then his nerve broke and he had to listen to himself scream. He screamed for three hours, and then the mayor came to look for him. When he had been dragged to safety with a rope, he was driven home and put to bed under sedatives. He must have babbled about the books, for the mayor, no doubt believing that running water is a barrier against witchcraft, locked them in a deserted cottage on the far side of the river.

"In a few days Desnos recovered, but decided that instead of going alone to fetch the books he would take with him an acquaintance from Souillac...a sensible choice of companion for I knew him well although he had a morbid interest in black magic. Desnos had a new car and was a most cautious driver, but when, after collecting the key of the cottage from the mayor, they were going down the steep hill to the river the brakes suddenly failed. The car hit the parapet of the bridge, overturned, and flung them into the water. Desnos suffered only minor damage, but my poor friend broke his right arm and both legs.

"In spite of his dreadful injuries he was so obsessed with the books that Desnos willingly agreed to leave

94

them in the cottage until he was sufficiently recovered for them to examine them together. I went to see him in hospital and offered to fetch the books so that he could enjoy them during his convalescence, but he rather brusquely refused my offer, saying that he preferred to wait until he could go himself and that I would hear in due course whether he wished me to negotiate their sale.

"I fear he even grudged sharing them with Desnos, for when he came out of hospital the archivist had just gone to Antibes for a fortnight's holiday, and yet, the very next day, he wrote to the mayor instructing him to send the books by train to Souillac. When the station-master telephoned to say the parcel had arrived, he, being still able only to hobble with crutches, sent his daughter to fetch it. Within half an hour she was at the station and hurried to the parcels office. But where was the parcel? Three clerks swore that a few moments earlier they had seen it on a shelf under the counter: the stationmaster made most exhaustive inquiries...one can well imagine the frenzied searching, the shouts, the accusations and denials. But nowhere was the parcel to be found.

"At last the poor girl returned home, by now in tears, distraught at the prospect of having to break such dreadful news to her father. But she did not have to tell him the books were lost. For when she entered the library, although he was sitting in the chair as she had left him, he was stone dead.

"The moment I heard the news, that same evening in fact, I wrote to Desnos telling him to cut short his holiday and return to carry out an intensive search for the missing parcel...being a bureaucrat himself I thought he might have some hope of getting action. The moment he received my letter he telegraphed to say he was catching the night train. But he did not catch it. On the way back from the telegraph office he went for a last bathe in the sea: and he drowned in three feet of water."

Chapter Twelve
HOW TO PLAY POST OFFICE

It was in St. Céré, to be exact in the sanctum of a private bank, that I witnessed a phenomenon then unique to me, although, so rapidly have conditions changed, that four years later it would have seemed commonplace. I watched the banker pick up the receiver of the telephone on his desk, give an Elysée number, and, a moment later, begin talking with his friend in Paris.

I would not have been more startled if the bud in his buttonhole had instantly become a rose in full bloom. For there had been no appreciable interval between his request and its fulfilment; no mounting crescendo of *"Allo! Allo!"*; no pitiful please to an obdurate operator of *"Ne couper pas, je vous en prie!"*

My amazement must have been obvious, for he said with a smile, "The telephones of St. Céré are doubtless under the benign guidance of the ghost of Monsieur Bourseul."

I failed to conceal that the significance of this remark eluded me; and, with the hint of rebuke such as might be deserved by someone who confessed to having never heard of Napoleon, he explained, with almost palpable pride, that Monsieur Charles Bourseul—surely I had not failed to notice his statue?—was the illustrious son of St. Céré who had invented the French telephone.

It was profoundly interesting to learn that these instruments, hanging in apparent innocence from their little brass hooks, and too fragile to receive the impact of thwarted venom, were not merely a malign sport of the species but an entirely different breed. The progenitor of this hydra died in 1912, yet his effigy has never been burned on a pyre of telegraph poles, nor his moppet sold with an outsize packet of pins. Instead, his statue, venerable in a frock coat, commands the Place Gambetta, opposite the establishment where I was gently taught—earlier schooling had occurred in other parts of the Lot—the more advanced moves of another gambit in Gallic communications, How-to-Play-Post-Office.

Though sharing a name with a frolic designed for children's parties, this game is suitable only for alert adults, and as a preliminary to learning the basic ploys one must realize that the most dominant and splendid characteristic of the French is that they are individualists, which is why the Germans, dedicated to the dreadful dogma of unquestioning obedience, are their natural enemies. So a French bureaucrat, whose fundamental instincts revolt against acting as a unit instead of as a person, conceals his feelings either by acting like a bully or being purposefully inefficient.

So unless you are by nature patient, or have an hour to spare, buy stamps, as the French do, at a tobacconist—easily identifiable by the red spindle-shaped sign which represents a 'carrot' of tobacco. But should you venture into a post office, remember that of the four or five officials in sight only one is likely to have sufficient herd-instinct to be a bureaucrat at heart. This Joiner is instantly recognizable, for she—the Joiner is nearly always female—is the only person on the far side of the counter who is doing any work. The other girls are too busy manicuring their nails or exchanging provocative remarks with the male employees to have time to notice the customers.

There are likely to be a few dispirited people standing, like sheep waiting to be dipped, behind an old man who is trying to draw his pension. He is offering a bundle of dog-eared papers to the Joiner, who either cannot, or will not, explain to him that as he has mislaid the necessary card he must fill up a form before he can be issued with a duplicate. Join this huddle and you are lost; or an hour is lost which you might have employed more pleasingly. You must catch the eye of one of the individualists who are amusing each other out of ear-shot.

This requires practice; the tyro is unlikely to produce any result. It is now that you must steadfastly resist the urge to raise your voice, to tap on the counter with a coin, to fidget while muttering audibly under your breath, or even grosser signs of exasperation such as staring at the clock or winding your wrist watch. Any such gestures would not only be discourteous; they would slow down the whole process, for everyone, including the Joiner, would stop to stare at you in astonishment. And why should they not stare? For they know, and will assume you have forgotten this basic fact, that time is *not* money. To be niggardly with time is the most unforgivable form of meanness. Argue over a franc if you must, and you may expect to be respected if not loved: but to be parsimonious about minutes is to become an outcast, and to be treated as such.

To cover your chagrin at the failure of your inexpert eye-catching exercises, enter into conversation with the other customers. Should shyness have crammed your mouth with sawdust, pretend that they are fellow-passengers in a railway carriage which has stopped alarmingly long in a tunnel, and so discover it to be your duty to make some jolly remark that may relieve the tension. If it is so early in the morning that no sip of cognac, no sup of wine, has yet awakened the French words which are oversleeping in some crevice of your mind, make friends with a dog. There is almost certain to be a dog there, and I have seen the most aloof of poodles become ecstatic when addressed as 'Bon Dog' by a retired colonel in tweeds. If you are not a dog lover you must make do by ingratiating yourself with a child.

Having now established yourself as one of the rare

beings whose foreignness is not a stigma of potential invader but a symbol of quality such as is borne by Scottish cashmere sweaters or penknives from Sheffield, the assembled company suddenly recognize that it is their duty to see that the courtesies of France are lavished upon you. By some subtle process of intuition, similar to the one which causes a murmuration of starlings to alter course, the counter is now lined with employees eager to serve you. The latest issue of stamps is produced from a drawer under the counter, for stamps are changed as often as a Parisienne changes her hats. It is expected that you will take thought before deciding which pictures you prefer as though you were brooding over a wine-list; so do not spoil the game by hurrying, or be put off your stroke by imagining that someone in the crowd behind you might have a train to catch. It is now only necessary to arrange your purchases in a decorative pattern on the envelope—it is more difficult to do this on a postcard without obscuring the address—to thank all the employees who, although they have not actually served you, have provided an audience, and to shake hands with each member of the admiring, if envious, crowd.

Having now passed your first test with flying colours you may, on a later day, set yourself the more arduous task of sending a telegram. I will make the problem easier by postulating that there is no one behind the counter save the Joiner. To gain her cooperation is not easy, but it can be achieved by using tactics such as would cause a paranoid watch-dog to accept you during its owner's absence. When you have at last wrung a reluctant smile from her, a crowd of people surges into the arena. Instantly her manner becomes glacial, for she sees you as a pupil who has tried to undermine her authority by being winsome with teacher during recess.

Angrily she seizes a telephone and embarks on an incomprehensible argument with an imaginary opponent. The aim is to make you feel guilty of eavesdropping until in acute embarrassment you shuffle away.

If you return to the attack, for now it is open warfare, without first gaining the cooperation of the majority of the audience, it requires no power of *déja vu* to forecast what will happen.

(a) You at last find a telegraph form, which will be in a box labelled something quite different.

(b) You decipher the instructions, if both your French and your eyesight are excellent.

(c) You fill up the form very clearly and carefully, in pencil, as no pen is provided and you have forgotten to bring your own.

(d) You tag on to the end of the queue and wait dispiritedly until at long last you can offer it to the Joiner.

(e) She adds up the words, tapping each with her pencil and counting out loud. Then she repeats the process, as though suspecting that an extra word is hiding and only waiting for her to take her eye off the rest to sidle into a gap and upset her calculations.

(f) She then asks you, in very rapid French, at what rate you wish to send it. *"Le plus vite,"* you say doggedly, for by now you have been so spendthrift with time that it would be pointless to economize with money. She darts meaningful glances at her sycophants which convey, "Regard the terrible extravagance of the English, who for years used to tell us that currency restrictions made them hoard their francs!" For customers from the United States her barb will be, "Consider the ostentation of the disgustingly rich Americans!"

(g) While the crowd stares at you she scrabbles through several cupboards and eventually unearths a tattered book in which she laboriously looks up the tariff. She then does elaborate sums on the back of an old envelope and announces the total. Victory seems within your grasp; but it is only a chimera. She looks again at the form, shrugs her shoulders to express "How can one cope with the idiocy of foreigners?" and explains loudly and slowly, so that the audience may realize you are judged to be deaf as well as mentally deficient, that you have deliberately wasted her time by writing in pencil when everyone knows that telegrams cannot be dispatched unless written clearly in ink. Should you have used ink she will employ the gambit that you have failed to use capital letters throughout, for the novice invariably puts 'and' or 'street' in script.

(h) The Joiner now crumples your carefully composed message and drops it disdainfully into her wastepaper basket. And you, as in the game of Snakes and Ladders, go back to the beginning and start all over again.

It is a comfort to know that after all these preliminaries the actual transmission of telegrams is very efficient and that letters flow to and fro from remote villages with alacrity. But something very mysterious happens to parcels. Early in June 1956 my publisher dispatched three parcels to me, by the same post from London, one containing the typescript, the other two being page-proofs of *Time Out of Mind.* I was with Madame Rochet at St. Cirq-Lapopie, which in this narrative I shall not reach until Chapter 17, and when the page-proofs arrived yet remained uncorrected because the typescript was missing, its absence became a subject of kind inquiry throughout the village.

Eventually I coped with the proofs without the typescript, and about a month later happened to mention its loss when chatting in the post office of St. Céré. It is a most delightful post office, and I had been accepted by the personnel almost as one of the family since spending two hours with them, during which work was suspended, while we stood in the doorway cheering the bicyclists who flashed past in the final spurt of a qualifying heat for the *Tour de France.*

"You have lost a parcel?" chorused the young man and the two pretty girls with whom I had so often gossiped. Suddenly they had become alert as bloodhounds. Had I filled in the form especially designed

101

for tracing parcels? I said I had not done so, and thought it must by now be so thoroughly lost that it had best be forgotten. But why did I think it was lost when it had been missing only for a month? To have searched for it earlier might have seemed unduly impatient, but now was the moment to fill in the relevant form, and by a benign chance they had one and would assist me to complete it correctly. This exercise, with the additional aid of some customers, I at last achieved—in itself a triumph for the questions were of extreme complexity and the space allotted to each answer no larger than a postage stamp.

A few days later I was playing billiards with Charles in the café where we had entertained the funambulists, when an urgent message was relayed to us from the Truite Dorée. Would we return at once to the hotel for there was a telephone call for us of the greatest urgency. Jostled by thoughts of disaster I ran down the street, and felt dizzy with relief to hear that the urgent call had not come from England but from Madame Rochet. She must have been waiting by the telephone, so rapidly were we connected. "You must come at once," she cried, "Tomorrow at the latest! At last it has arrived! Your parcel! It came last night, by goods train! Imagine my indignation when I was told...I made them admit it...that for all this time it has been hiding from the whole village, in the parcels office run by the cretins who occupy the station of Toulouse!"

No one was ever able to explain why a parcel sent by post should arrive, without extra charge, by goods train. Or why it should overshoot its mark by a hundred miles before languishing in some reedy backwater of the transport system. This is just one of the inexplicable things which happen to parcels when they weigh more than a kilo; and even the London Library was defeated by the French parcels system, for a book they posted to me on the third of May arrived on the fourteenth of September.

Chapter Thirteen
ON PRIESTS AND PLUMBING

Although in the Lot the conflict between Catholic and Huguenot did not result in such wholesale massacres as were inspired by Catherine de Medici in more northerly parts of France, differences in dogma provided an excuse for sanguinary feuds comparable to the more violent phases of Scottish clan warfare. But in the case of Montal and Assier during the latter part of the fifteenth century, although Jehanne de Balzac, Dame de Montal, was a staunch Catholic, and Jeanne de Galiot de Genoillac, Dame d'Assier, so passionate a convert to the Huguenot cause that Calvin frequently accepted her hospitality, the two women preferred to ignore each other rather than risk destruction of their properties.

The Château d'Assier is 30 kilometres from St. Céré by D.48 through Leyme to Lacapelle Marival, then south on N.140 (the main St. Céré-Figeac road), and west on N.653. It was built by the Dame d'Assier's father, Jacques de Galiot de Genoillac, with part of the fortune he accumulated while Grand Armourer and Minister of Finance to François Premier. Only the west wing now remains, but a print in the Bibliothéque Nationale shows that in 1680 it was as richly decorated as and even larger than Montal. The church he built at Assier is still intact, and contains his splendidly flamboyant tomb surmounted by his statue, leaning on a gun barrel with his foot on a cannon ball. For Galiot de Genoillac was the militarist who completely revolutionized battle tactics by employing artillery. The outside of the church is surrounded by a frieze in high relief, a strip-cartoon describing one of his campaigns in which cannon reduce castles which also bristle with cannon, perhaps to point the moral that as massive walls were now useless for defence against the new weapon, everyone had better follow his example and build houses of elegance that were comfortable to live in.

When Charles and I first went to Assier we returned to St. Céré by N.140 because we wanted to stop on the way to visit the château at Aynac. It is a curious structure, for the central donjon is six stories high and at each corner there is a round tower with a roof shaped like a sugar-sifter which increases the resemblance to a gigantic cruet. It had recently been acquired by the State as a holiday home for disabled seamen, but I had been told that three of the rooms had chimney-pieces and ceilings classified as national monuments, which therefore had to be shown to visitors on request.

However we did not see them, although the château was empty except for a caretaker. She was in an exceedingly bad temper, as we discovered when she leaned out of an upper window to brandish a broom at us. "The sailors arrive tomorrow and I am busy, so go away!" she shouted. We tried to mollify her, and when this failed we left, considerably disgruntled. We should probably never have gone to Aynac again unless a timely cloudburst had driven us into the hotel.

"So you have been turned away from the Château," said Madame la Patronne indignantly as she poured wine for us in the bar which is also the dining-room and the kitchen. "That monster of a woman is not, as of course you understand, of Aynac. She was inflicted on us by the new owners. She comes from Paris."

Knowing that 'to come from Paris' can sometimes to the Lotoise seem as opprobrious as to come from 'the black North' to the Southern Irish, we made appropriately sympathetic noises.

"How different it was when the real family lived there!" she said, picking up a glass and polishing it vigorously. "But the last of them died...such a kind, generous lady she was too—at the clinic of Figeac during the war." She sighed. "Poor lady, she never really recovered after her daughter was shot."

"Shot by the Germans?"

"No, not by the Germans," she said after an uneasy pause: and to prevent further questions she bustled over to the stove and pretended that the soup required her full attention. It was excellent soup, which in the Lot is unusual, and the prelude to so good a dinner that we went back there several times, for a meal including wine for the two of us never cost more than twenty shilling.

It was not that evening, nor from her that we heard about the tragedy at the château, but while gossiping with some of her 'regulars'. It was explained to us that there would have been no tragedy if the repairs to the electric light machine at the château had not been entrusted to a foreign firm—'foreign' meaning that the firm came neither from St. Céré nor Figeac. The electrician fell in love with the daughter of Madame la Marquise, a young lady, very *bien élevée,* who of a certainty had given him no encouragement. In fact the only time she was overheard to speak to him it was to tell him not to be impertinent. But the electrician had a revolver...opinion was divided as to whether he had acquired it while working with the Resistance or purchased it later on the black-market. One day he waylaid the girl and declared his passion. He was repulsed. And fired five bullets into her. The assassin would have been lynched, so we were vehemently assured, had he not cheated the village of its vengeance by killing himself with the sixth bullet.

As though this were not tragedy enough, the Curé then disgraced himself by falling in love with the bereaved mother, and was so ashamed of doing so that he hanged himself from a tree in her park. But he could not even hang himself properly, and was cut down just in time to save his life, though his face was purple as an over ripe fig and his eyes bulged like a bull-frog's. We were asked to imagine the idiocy of such an act, especially as no word of love had passed his lips and no one would have guessed his feelings unless he had bleated his impious thoughts while his rescuers were helping him to get his breath back.

At this juncture everyone joined in with indignant memories of the Curé. Their major grievance seemed to be that listening to their confessions had not given him a more robust attitude towards sin, and that a priest who could not keep his own thoughts to himself was an unreliable repository of other people's secrets.

I was about to ask what happened to the unfortunate man, when one of our companions loosed a great belly-laugh and said: "We were glad to be rid of him; and we let him know it, before he fled from Aynac at dawn the following morning."

I felt acutely sorry for the poor little cleric, who was the victim of a dogma which professes to be Christian and yet considers celibacy a suitable discipline for a man whose duty it should be to cure souls by teaching his people how to love their neighbours and themselves. But while I was searching my limited vocabulary for words in which to put forward this point of view, the man on the other side of me launched with gusto into a story about the Curé of another Lotoise village.

One morning this Curé assembled his congregation, took off his cassock, and announced that he could not celebrate the Mass as he had fallen in love with the village school-teacher, and that after he had renounced his vows he would marry her. And marry her he did, for the mayor could not refuse to perform a civil ceremony. When they came out of the Mairie as man and wife the village street was deserted, but they walked hand in hand towards the café at which they invited the villagers to drink their health.

Suddenly every window was flung open: stones and

dung rained down upon them. There were a great many stones. As they lay stunned and bleeding in the roadway an ambulance drew up beside them. The plot had been meticulously planned and the ambulance summoned on a fake emergency call so as to arrive at the exact moment that would relieve the villagers from any obligation of aiding their victims...who spent their wedding night and many more nights also, in Cahors hospital.

The last time Charles and I had dinner at Aynac, Madame la Patronne asked me to see the bedrooms so that I could decide which one I preferred when we returned to visit her. There are six bedrooms in the Hotel Peyrudan and each had a newly installed basin and bidet with hot and cold running water. "The bidets were very expensive," said Madame with feeling. "I almost persuaded myself to the further extravagance of a bathroom, but this would have been foolish for a bath is seldom used and makes too great a demand on the hot water."

"A bathroom is more popular with English visitors than any number of bidets," I suggested tentatively. "In England a bidet is a rarity."

She looked startled, and then exclaimed: "For a moment I did not realize you were making a joke. No bidets indeed! Everyone knows the English are fussy about cleanliness, so how could anyone be silly enough to imagine that you were serious when you pretended they only wash their hands and faces!"

I went into each bedroom, debating aloud for her benefit whether I preferred the colour of the curtains in one to the view from another, opening cupboards and bouncing on beds, which pleased her exceedingly. For not to look at every available room before making your choice is as incomprehensible, and as discourteous, to a French *hoteliére* as it would be to say, "Any bottle will do" when offered a wine-list.

I had made my final choice and we were in the

corridor when she asked, "I am now going to ask you a most important question. Do the English prefer to sit or to stand?"

For a moment I thought she was asking whether to invest in bar stools. Then she flung open a door to reveal the kind of W.C.—now fortunately less prevalent in the Lot, in which it is necessary to perch precariously on two foot-rests. Like the rest of the hotel, this one was clean, but I noticed an extra hazard in three brooms which were balanced on a narrow ledge above high-tide level. "Do you prefer to sit or to stand?" she repeated anxiously.

"We sit," I said firmly.

"But why, Madame? Why?"

My French withered as I tried to be helpful and tactful at the same time. Phrases skeltered through my mind....Because it is so difficult holding my bag in my teeth....Because I get cramp in my calves....Because one has to be as agile as a sparrow balancing on a telephone wire....I discarded these arguments as being too difficult except in English and heard myself saying pontifically, "We sit because we also read here. In England it is the custom."

"Read!" she exclaimed. "The English *read* in the W.C.?"

I felt even more idiotic. "It is because we are shy. We do not like to admit, even to ourselves, why we go to this little room...so we read to take our minds off the subject."

She looked completely mystified. "The English are shy of going to the W.C.? But they are not shy of being seen eating their dinner, and surely one is as natural as the other?"

"I know it is. But many of my compatriots *don't* know." I must have said this very earnestly, for she stopped smiling and became thoughtful. "Madame, you have done me a great service, for without your help I should have continued to offend my English clients."

She beat her forehead with the palm of her hand. "I blush to think how I misunderstood an English lady who came to lunch with us only last week. If I had not been so ignorant she might still have been here, and you could have apologized to her for my stupidity. You ask me what I did?"

I had not had time to do so, but she forgave this oversight and paused only long enough to increase the tension of her narrative. "This English lady—I know she is English for when I look down from the balcony I see there is a G.B. on the car—is with her husband. I know he is her husband for he is too brusque with her to be a lover or even a friend. He is having a drink at the bar when she whispers to me that she wishes to wash her hands. Why does she not wear glasses, I ask myself, if she is too blind to see that the wash basin is placed most conveniently on the wall behind her. I point to the wash basin but she shakes her head. I think that she is complaining that the roller towel is not clean enough, so I fetch a fresh one from the cupboard. Again she shakes her head. Surely she cannot be complaining about the soap? Does she expect me to provide a new piece for each client? But I give her a new piece, and still she is not satisfied. Then she says to me, 'Can I go *upstairs?*' Naturally I think she wishes to inspect the bedrooms before deciding whether she wishes to stay in my hotel. I show her them all...except Number Five which is occupied by a commercial traveller from Toulouse. None of them seem to please her. I am beginning to feel indignant that she has not even had the civility to inquire my prices when suddenly she sees this door, on which W.C. is so clearly painted, and bolts inside as though it were a burrow and she a hunted rabbit."

"The poor woman wished to make peepee but was too shy to say so. I told you the English are shy," I said apologetically.

"Oh, my dear Madame, how grateful I am to you! I must go immediately to tell my husband."

She rushed off to find him, and I seized the opportunity to retreat into the object of our discussion. I was wary of the brooms but not wary enough, for one of them toppled from its ledge and struck me a shrewd blow on the back of the head while I was leaping to avoid the inundation which, as is usual in such situations, resulted from the most cautious tweak at the plug.

After the protracted farewells that followed our admirable dinner, Madame la Patronne leaned over the rail of the balcony and shouted: "Tell all your English friends that they will be happy in my hotel. Not a moment's shyness shall they suffer. I shall tell them at once, 'The room for *reading* is at the top of the stairs!'"

Chapter Fourteen
MIDSUMMER MAGIC

The Causse de Gramat lies above the escarpment of the Lotoise reaches of the Dordogne and extends southwards to the gorges of the Célé and the Lot. A causse is a limestone plateau, which offers an abrupt change of scenery to that of the fertile valleys and forested hills. Dry-stone walls abound where there is sufficient depth of soil to have justified the labour of clearing the boulders from the arid little fields, and the woodland is of stunted oak or juniper.

On the north-west of this causse is the famous shrine of Roc Amadour. In the Middle ages it may have been miraculous and the superimposed churches clinging to the face of a sheer precipice are still impressive, if viewed from a sufficient distance. But actually to enter the place is to find it so ruthlessly restored, so vampired with hotels and restaurants and cafés and souvenir shops that it is acutely repugnant, even when not inundated with tourists.

Only slightly less advertised but far less disappointing is the Gouffre de Padirac, 17 kilometres by N.673 from Roc Amadour. Here commercialization although rife is more benign, for instead of having to plod down some 500 feet to the bottom of the enormous pot-hole, lifts now descend to the rock-fault which leads to the illuminated underground river. Along this you glide in a punt, and disembark to follow a path beside a descending staircase of small lakes, overhung with stalactites, to reach the largest cavern. Here even the most claustrophobic citizen would feel at ease, for the roof soars to 270 feet and each turn of the narrow path, each vantage point gained by rock-cut steps or spidery iron bridge, makes it seem yet more improbable that nature has produced this superb phantasia without the assistance of Mr. Disney.

If Padirac has whetted your appetite for caves there are other notables in the neighborhood, which is riddled with temptations for the speleologist. There is the Grotte de Presque, 6 kilometres along N.673 from St. Céré; another at Lacave, on the Dordogne, 10 kilometres by D.43 to the south-east of Souillac; and the Grottes de Cougnac, 3 kilometres on N.704 northwest of Gourdon. But the best in the Lot, for it has cave paintings only outclassed by those at Lascaux, is the Grotte du Pech Merle, near Cabrerets on the river Célé.

But before going south of the Causse de Gramat go back to Carennac by D.20, for this road offers superb views northwards across the Dordogne valley, especially in the light of early evening when the Tours de St. Laurent flares like a torch on its height, and Castelnau-Bretenoux glows in the distance like a great rose.

The roofscape, of stone tiles shaped like fish-scales and gilded with lichen, is one of the joys of Carennac, for many of the houses are contemporary with the monastery which was founded in the twelfth century. The château was originally part of the monastic buildings and it was there, between 1681 and 1695, that the benign Abbé Fénelon wrote *Télémaque*. It is now a hotel, where Charles and I spend a few days before moving to the Truite Dorée, and it adjoins the church which is deservedly renowned for the tympanum of the west door. Inside the church there is an even more moving *mise-en-tombeau* of the sixteenth century. Nicodemus and Joseph of Arimathea hold the shroud on which a Jesus at peace is lying as though asleep, while his mother and three Marys and John grieve for his body.

On Sunday, 24th June, 1956, I spent most of the day proof-correcting in the garden of the Hotel du Château, which I mention only because anyone who has corrected proofs knows that this niggling job is in no way

Above: Mise-en-tombeau found in church at Carennac
Below: Twelfth-century tympanum over west door

conducive to an awareness of ghosts. About six o'clock I felt a sudden urge to go to the church, which I had briefly visited the day before, but only as a dutiful tourist. I resisted the impulse, for my inclination was to finish the proofs, stick them in an envelope, have a drink and look forward to dinner. However the illogical urge persisted. I went to look for Charles and found him asleep, such an unusual daytime occurence that I tiptoed out of the room and tried to engross myself on the terrace in a detective story.

"Go to the church...go to the church..." became an insistent beat which made nonsense of the printed words I was trying to register with my mind. I felt resentful. Why should I go spook-hunting when I had been plodding at proofs all day?...I did not feel in the mood for spook-hunting....

Crossly I marched down the long gallery, across the dining-room, opened the bedroom door, announced, "I am going to the church," banged the door, and went there.

The church was empty. I walked briskly down the aisle and stood staring at the *mise-en–tombeau*. I was obedient but still feeling resentful. What business was it of mine that the sculptor had used his dead son as a model for the dead Christ? The boy had probably died of tuberculosis, but so had a lot of other men's sons. He had begun the carving when he knew the boy was dying, and finished it as the boy lay dead. The other figures were added later. The men holding the shroud by which they were lowering the body into the tomb were self-portraits. The original carving was in wood, much smaller than this one...small enough to be carried on the back of a donkey. It was on a donkey when he took it from monastery to monastery until he found a prior who would allow him to carve it in stone. But why? Why?

He thinks his son died because his prayers were not offered to the right god. He thinks that had he prayed to the god of the Christians his son would have been permitted to live...If the Christian god demands prayers for the souls of the dead before they can enter heaven, then his son must have prayers. Monks pray to statues of their god. If they see his son in the semblance of their god they will pray to it; and it will be as though they said the Mass for his son's soul....

After the sculptor had wrought, and after many years had passed, this did he confess, he being then an old man and dying, to a priest of Carennac. And the priest, being not a Christian except that his dogma usurped that title, cursed him.

Charles, who in fact was wearing rope-soled sandals and made no sound, now came down the aisle to stand behind me, but to me it seemed that he tramped in hob-nailed boots. Silently he opened a notebook, and to my ears the pages clattered like sheets of corrugated iron. Through this cacophony I could just hear the priest endlessly repeating the curse..."And so that my condemnation shall endure beyond your hopes of salvation I prison you also in Time: so that your release may not, and cannot, and shall not come until one who knows the Old Religion of the Fire, and still the older Religion of the Moon, and the Religion behind the New Religion, shall, for no reason except the love in his heart, approach you who are circumscribed as I am, as all men are who offer, if they even offer so much, only their intellect, their courage and their gold."

At last I knew my duty. And hear Joan's voice declare: "The omens are propitious: I am here!"

And heard the prelate answer, "Who are you, heathen?"

"A person lively on my master's business."

"Your name?"

"My friends: I have no other."

"A mendicant friar!"

"No, my impoverished sir, a woman: but kindly, having learned kindliness in my master's service.

115

"Then leave my church!"

"I take no orders when I find a friend whose forehead would feel easier for my hands."

"Go, woman! Go!"

"In company I will go, in my own time. Come with me, my good friend."

"I cannot! I cannot!..."

"Yes, come with me. For in my hand flows warm blood into my urgent veins, which for your resurrection have been given us to share."

The prelate must now have seen me as the sculptor whom he cursed: for it was, as always, the one who curses and not the one who is cursed who is imprisoned, for he hurls at me, "He is not Christ but your son!"

"How else has man, or woman, since this earth began seen God, save in the likeness of their love? What else is God? What else is our Christ...unless the emblem be monstrously distorted, save that we see in Him our dearest love more clearly than aforetime?"

"But I am dead! Dead as my wood and stone and wit and brain!"

"No, sir, you boast. Your forehead pulses with blood under my hands; the skin is warm; your flesh as warm as mine. Rise up and come with me into the air; and love and laugh and seek the place of friends, and there find Christ. And I will take your sorrow and your fear, and throw them like bright birds into the air.

"Why should I do so? In gratitude that you have known the same sweet magic. Bless you, my love. And with you from this life take only your most excellent nobility. And leave the rest; as rust on an iron altar, as stone that splits, as wood that ants can kill. But to you in this moment when our hearts are one with God, feeling but love for each other, I say to you, 'Go free: in peace: in love: in God—whose symbol of love is Christ.'"

In the garden after dinner, watching the full moon

rise through the branches of a catalpa tree to flood the river with light, Charles said contentedly, "I knew you were on the beam the moment you declaimed, 'The omens are propitious!'"

"That is the only bit which I still don't understand. What omens?"

"The coincidence of the major Christian and pagan festivals. Today is the Feast of St. John, the day of St. John's fires, which were originally the Beltane fires of the midsummer festival of the Old Religion—a term which embraces any religious system prior to the Christian dogma. A sphere expanding from its centre was their symbol of spiritual evolution; hence the sun at noonday or the full moon were their symbol of worship."

He paused to look long at the full moon, and then said, "I regret there are no facilities here for lighting a ritual fire as we used to do, even though the job for which we were sent here has already been done."

The moon was now so bright that we could see the folded hills on the far side of the valley. Suddenly a crest was pricked with light which steadily grew stronger. "It's increasing too fast to be a house burning," exclaimed Charles. "I wonder...Yes! They *are* lighting the midsummer fires! Look! There's another one...and another!"

And as we watched the beaconed heights became an altar to the Company of the Gods.

Chapter Fifteen
FORTRESS WITHOUT FOES

To take the main road, N.703, when going from
Carennac to Martel would be as unimaginative as to
select only potato salad from a fine hors d'oeuvre. For
D.43 on the left bank of the Dordogne winds below the
semicircle of heather pink cliffs, the Cirque de
Montvalent, and by crossing the river at Gluges there
are lovely valley vistas as N.681 winds up the escarpment to approach from the best angle Martel's splendid fortress church.

When Denys and I were there the great porch was
lively with martins swooping down from their nests in
the groined roof, and the sough of their wings seemed
an appropriate accompaniment for the joyous angels
which attend the gentle Christ in Judgement above the
lovely Romanesque doorway. I already had affectionate memories of this sleepy little town, with its seven
towers, its sixteenth-century town hall, its market-
place and medieval houses encircled by a wide street
that marks the site of the walls which guarded it when
Henry Courtmantle died here after sacking Roc
Amadour; but, until I went there in May, I did not
realize that Martel could boast such an exuberance of
roses. Lavender is distilled here, and also the walnut
liqueur called Noix, and the local truffles are claimed
to be finer even than the truffles of Perigueux, so it is
not surprising that one eats well and sleeps comfort-
ably at the Lion d'Or.

It is only 15 kilometres by N.703 to Souillac, but D.23
winds back to the river to follow it to Creysse, the
drowsy village where, dining pleasurably under the
plane trees of the Restaurant de l'Isle, I expected to see

a herd of cows cross the ancient bridge over a back-water of the Dorodogne until I realized that the incidental music was provided not by approaching cow-bells but by an orchestra of frogs.

St. Sozy is the next village downstream, and here take D.15, unless you want to visit the caves at Lacave, in which case cross the river and follow the left bank, and afterwards cross it again by the bridge below the Château de Montal.

The Romanesque church of Sainte Maries at Souillac resulted, so it was widely believed in the twelfth century, from a pact between the devil and a monk called Théophile, who was granted the power to build it for the price of his soul. This pact is immortalized in carvings above the original west door, which is now inside the church, having been transferred there two hundred years ago during alterations to the west façade. Théophile can be seen handing the signed deeds to Satan, and swearing fealty by placing his hands between the hands of his overlord; and also depicted is the happy ending to his story when, after dedicating his church to the Virgin Mary she flew down from heaven to snatch back the deed and return it to her faithful servitor.

But before this benign intervention Théophile must have been acutely aware of the future he envisaged, and as though the current concepts of hell were insufficient he also distorted the pagan gods further to point his moral. Satan is shown as a skeleton with the head of Pan, who here is not the symbol of the spirit's evolution through animal to man, but the source of panic terror. The Seven Deadly Sins are equally horrific; but there is one carving not inspired by fear—the pillar of the doorway, honoured among sculptors, the vividly alive, ecstatic dancing Isaiah.

From Souillac go south for 20 kilometres on N.20, and then, soon after Payrac, turn west on to N.673 which in another 57 kilometres, through Gourdon and

Cazals, brings you to the hamlet of St. Martin-le-Redon where D.158 leads up to the magnificent castle of Bonaguil.

Bonaguil is much more than a castle; it is a man's hopes and his fears transmuted into stone. The man was Bérenger de Roquefeuil, who was born in 1448 when already the bastions of the Middle Ages were being swept aside by the glittering tide of the Renaissance. He was five when the Hundred Years War came to an end, leaving the English with Calais as a last outpost of the slowly dwindling possessions which three centuries earlier had been greater than those ruled over by the King of France.

It was no longer fashionable to build castles which, realists had already recognized, were becoming impracticable since the increasing employment of cannon. Châteaux were much more comfortable to live in; and why build new castles when nearly every hill was already so crowned in protection of its village?

If Bérenger had wished simply to live in a castle, he owned many from which to choose, for his lands stretched from Carcassonne to Perigord, making him one of the richest landowners of France. But, like a child clinging to the protection of its nursery, he could feel secure only if he could convince himself that times were not changing. Castles on which artillery were brought to bear were no longer impregnable. But a castle built in a narrow valley, where invaders would be within bow-shot if they attempted to haul cannon into range: that would be a very different proposition! To guard against frontal attack the Keep should not be square, nor even round, but shaped like the prow of a boat so that cannon balls would glance harmlessly aside. But he would have a round Keep too, taller and wider and stronger than any yet built, over a hundred feet high with six storeys, and walls ten feet thick!

For four years he designed and redesigned his dream on parchment, considered and reconsidered which

120

site would best suit his need, and at last, perhaps rather reluctantly, decided that the only one which fulfilled all his requirements was in an obscure corner of his domain where it would serve no useful purpose, especially as there was a small castle there already, save his own protection.

Did he at this juncture, being now twenty-nine, have a twinge of doubt that it was seemly for the "Noble, magnificent and mighty Lord, Bérenger de Roquefeuil, Lord and Baron of Roquefeuil, of Blanquefort, of Castelnau, of Combret, of Roquefére, Count of Nants," to take quite so much care of himself instead of looking after his people? If conscience nagged he did his best to drown its irritant voice with a bold fanfare, "By my Lord Jesus and all the saints of His glorious Paradise, I will create such a castle as shall never be taken by those who owe me their fealty, or by the English—should they have the audacity to return, or by the most powerful armies of the King of France."

It is significant that his first defiance is directed against his own people, who may well have regretted that he was not cast in the same mould as his father, who, although he embroiled them in battles, could be relied upon during more tranquil periods to protect them from marauders and rival serf-owners. Was it a sense of inadequacy which on the one hand drove him to construct such an imperishable carapace and on the other caused him to write, on 19th December, 1503, "My poor state of health is now so apparent that everyone knows that I am usually ill, especially during the past two years, and am unable to regain my strength because of the damp chills which afflict my belly and brain."

To add to his troubles one of his baronies, Castelnau-Montraitier, refused to pay their taxes. He tried to subdue them, but sent such an inadequate force that it was routed by the townspeople. Incensed by this rebellion he sent a much stronger band of men-at-arms from his estate in Rouergue. These troops too were routed, and had to take refuge in his castle at Sauverterre; which the men of Castelnau besieged, took by assault, pillaged, and then demolished.

When news of this appalling indignity was brought to Bérenger he weakly decided to abandon the struggle to uphold his authority, no doubt fearing that vengeance on the rebels would arouse such widespread hatred that he would lose the other revenues he needed for the building of Banoguil. He might have been able to pretend, at least to himself, that his inaction was inspired by clemency, but he was deprived even of this solace; for the people of Castelnau appealed to Parliament at the Court of Toulouse, who, on 20th July, 1493, gave judgement against Bérenger and ordered him to pay three hundred pounds damages. And pay this he did, being unable to withstand even the threat of the King's displeasure.

This humiliation was too great to be endured except in the seclusion of his great castle, to which he retreated never again to emerge, and on which he lavished all his energies until, twenty years later, even he could not dream another dream to translate to stone. Now at last he was ready to defy anyone who questionsd his authority! Now let the King besiege him!

Slowly ten years passed by: but no one except servitors came up the narrow valley; no one accepted the mute challenge of those soaring walls.

Bérenger de Roquefeuil must have been far more robust than he had feared when young, for he lived to be eighty-two—a great age in his century. His last testament is dated the ninth day of January 1530: "...No one living in the flesh can avoid the terrible judgement of God, before whom he must render full and complete reason for his acts: so, when nothing is more certain than his death, and nothing more uncertain than his next hour, the wise man does not defer commands which concern his soul, his body, his personal possessions and his lands."

His tomb was already waiting for him in the church of Saint Michael de Bonaguil. Now he gave instructions that his body was to be put into it...."neither with a pall of cloth-of-gold, nor hearse, nor torches, nor funerary candles, nor pennants of the coats of arms of my nobility. But there shall be present one hundred and twenty priests or clerics of churches of good fame, to pray for my soul."

Meticulously as he had planned the background of his living until the background became the fabric of his life, so did he set the stage for his dying. Now there was no one to wait for except death: and he was too courteous to keep death waiting. So the next day he died.

The castle at Bonaguil

Chapter Sixteen
LANDSCAPE FOR BANNERS

When Charles and I went to Villeneuve-sur-Lot, which is 34 kilometres southwest of Bonaguil by N.111, we intended to spend only one night there on our way up-river from Bordeaux. But we were so comfortable at the Hotel Gache that we lingered for the first week of June, and returned to an even warmer welcome from Madame Gache that August. Should you be a light sleeper, even when lulled by her admirable meals, ask for a room overlooking the courtyard, for however much one has enjoyed looking at the renowned fruit and vegetables blazoning the stalls of the lovely market square, one feels less romantic about them when lorries taking them to Paris grind through the narrow streets soon after dawn.

Precipitous steps lead down from the Old Bridge to the water's edge where, in the sunlight, patient anglers drowse; but if you explore the riverside path at night, as I did on my first evening, keep sufficiently alert to hear a window open far above you. For the casement in one of the ancient houses, which cling to the cliff-face like swallows' nests, will not be opening wide on faerie lands forlorn except to disgorge the contents of a household bucket. But such hazards are of minimal importance, compared to the pleasure of getting close to the sound and surge of the moonlit weir.

Villeneuve-sur-Lot was one of the new towns which were built entire, instead of developing haphazardly round the core of a castle or monastery, when this part of France was under beneficent Plantagenet rulership during the twelfth and thirteenth centuries. These bastides, the contemporary name which some of them still retain, have a grid of streets enclosed by a circular defensive wall pierced by four towered gates—this basic plan sometimes being modified to suit the local terrain. At the centre is the market-place, containing a paved platform under a pillared roof and surrounded by cloisters which support the upper floors of houses. The church, also near the centre of the town, is strongly fortified, so that it can serve the same purpose as does the Keep in a castle's defence works.

Bastides have a much greater significance than merely being a startling innovation in the development of town planning, for they were designed to house and protect a new storey of society, which for centuries had consisted of a ground floor of nobility and an attic of clerics poised uneasily above a basement of serfs. Through the ethics promulgated by Eleanor of Aquitaine a new level of the social structure now became important. This was the middle class, largely composed of men who had been serfs until it was recognized that serfs might become a profitable investment if given the status of freemen, who could produce revenue for their former owners. The land necessary to feed the population of a bastide, the tools and materials for its dwelling houses, and the construction of the town wall and its defences, were provided either by the Crown or by a private landowner. He, in return, received ten percent of the production, in cash or in kind, from every male who lived there. But this tithe was not levied on a serf until he had been free for seven years, during which time he must build a house on the plot assigned to him, completing the first storey before the end of his second year, and learn a trade or craft by which to support himself and his family who, in the interim period, had been maintained by the bastide's overlord.

Bastides developed a fervent civic pride, but, except during the Wars of Religion, the rivalry between them was similar to that enjoyed by opposing factions at a Cup

Final. For instance, the Duc de Sully recounts in his Memoires how Villefranche-du-Perigord raided Monpazier, on a night of 1576, to find the gates unguarded and so few men in the town that they carried off a quantity of booty with surprising ease. In good heart they tramped the eight miles home, being unaware that the men of Monpazier were following a parellel path on their way back from an equally unopposed foray. Both teams were received by infuriated women who could be pacified only by calling the match a draw and returning every stolen object to its rightful owner.

Monpazier, its mellow stone glowing in the sunlight like newrun honey, is 44 kilometres northeast of Villeneuve-sur-Lot by N.676 and D.104, and on the way there are Montflanquin and Villereal, both bastides well worth exploring. The Château de Biron is 8 kilometres to the south of Monpazier and you will have seen it in the distance from several angles for it commands the landscape.

I first went to Biron with Charles in June, when the place was deserted except for the caretaker and his young son who were bottling off wine from the château vineyard. Charles joined them in this pleasing occupation, while I wandered through echoing rooms in search of the Duc de Biron's ghost, who is said to haunt the staircase carrying his head under his arm in protest against his execution for treason by Henri IV. Although the conditions were ideal I found no sniff of a spook, nor was I able to reconstruct, except in the pallid terms of intellect, the purposeful bustle which must have occurred in the enormous kitchen, with its original ovens and ranks of charcoal heated warming shelves, when the Duke of his father, who too was a Marshal of France, dispensed their lavish sixteenth-century hospitality.

I then went to the Renaissance chapel on the ramparts of the outer courtyard, but here again I felt nothing but pleasure in its architecture, and this pleasure somewhat diminished because it was cluttered with scaffolding, being in process of restoration by the Beaux Arts, and now contains only copies of its most famous treasures—a Descent from the Cross and a *Mise en Tombeau,* for the originals are in the Metropolitan Museum of New York. The chapel is built directly above another one whose entrance is outside the château gate. This is dark and dank, and one of the villagers told me that his grandfather refused to attend Mass there because he objected to his prayers having to ascend through a sieve of the nobility before they could become audible to God.

The second time I went there was with my daughter Gillian and her husband, David Wynne, when they came to join us that August. I had told them about the tranquillity of Biron and how restful it was to wander through it alone, so it was unfortunate that our arrival coincided with three coach-loads of hot and disgruntled tourists, with whom they were herded round the castle while I spent a comparatively peaceful hour contemplating a magnificent bignonia which hung the wall of the gate-house with carillons of copper bells.

To the south and southeast of Villeneuve-sur-Lot the landscape has the magical quality sometimes found in the background of medieval tapestries, for there are walled hilltop towns, particularly Laroque, Puymirol and Tournon d'Agenais, from which it would seem perfectly contemporary to see a lady from the Courts of Love ride out with her troubadours or to hear a fanfare's silver.

In June, the fields on the steep slopes look as though they were spread with banners, for wild flowers growing among the young crops show as patches of solid colour when seen from this unfamiliar angle, and each species is sharply divided from the one growing in the neighbouring plot, so that a rectangle of poppy scarlet may adjoin one of vivid violet sage, or a panel of pink centaury be set between wide borders of cornflower blue and toadflax yellow.

Charles and I were driving past Montaigu-de-Quercy, 30 kilometres east-south-east of Villeneuve-sur-Lot, when I noticed that the village streets were strewn with rushes. "The procession will start in a few minutes," we were told excitedly when we went into the café for a drink, so we decided to stay to see what it was all about. Half an hour passed, during which the shutters of all the houses were closed and the façades draped with white sheets and table cloths, to which bunches of flowers, some real, some of paper, had been pinned. We decided to explore, and found groups of women decorating altars, which had been erected in three side streets and in the open space before the church at the crest of the village...it was not until later that we realized that these sites represented the four cardinal points.

"The procession will start any minute now," said an old man who came out of his house to join us, perhaps feeling we might be getting restive after waiting an hour at the vantage point in front of the church to which we had been directed. With some difficulty he sat down beside us and then pulled up the leg of his trouser to show us his wooden leg. The leg still hurt him although it had been cut off by a shell splinter in 1914, a disaster which he related with exceedingly vivid detail. Suddenly the church doors swung open, and a double file of little girls in white emerged into the brilliant sunshine and advanced towards the altar, singing in a high clear treble that sounded like the twittering of birds.

Behind them came a palanquin supported on four stout poles, each with two bearers, stalwart villagers dressed in Sunday black. It was curtained with yellow brocade and the canopy had a tuft of yellow ostrich feathers at each corner which made it look like a four-poster bed. We thought it contained a votive statue until we noticed that beneath it a pair of trousered legs was keeping in step with the bearers, who set it rever-

128

ently down by the temporary altar. The curtains were then drawn back to reveal a robed and mitred bishop, who dismounted with dignity, although his ecclesiastical vehicle stood so high off the ground that this required the same agility as stepping over a lawn-tennis net.

The congregation, most of whom were women all dressed in black, had followed the procession from the church and formed a semicircle, facing the bishop who was now seated in a secular arm chair from which he addressed the assembled company. The theme of his discourse remains obscure for we could hear only an undulant murmur. He then rose to his feet and delivered a Latin prayer, while the people knelt and were afterwards lavishly sprinkled with holy water. The bishop then took off his spectacles, polished them with his handkerchief, and again entered the confines of his palanquin, which this time led the procession while the little girls, whose attention had strayed, were chivvied back into line by three agitated nuns.

We were about to follow the crowd when Charles noticed two old women who were trying to carry the bishop's arm-chair down a flight of precipitous stone steps. It was obviously too heavy for them and they thankfully accepted his assistance, panting out that they had only taken this difficult short cut because the chair must reach the next altar before the bishop did so.

By exerting every ounce of his considerable strength Charles managed to achieve this feat single-handed, although on one particularly steep and slippery slope of cobbles he lost his footing and it seemed only too probable that he would complete the journey using the chair as a sledge. However, all went well and the chair was safely in position before the palanquin came round the corner. Charles's gesture was appreciated, for after the procession had disbanded we received much kindly hospitality before we were allowed to depart.

Chapter Seventeen
THE BEAUTIFUL VILLAGE

On the day of early June when Charles and I left Villeneuve-sur-Lot we lunched at the Restaurant du Midi in Tournon d'Agenais, and then, contentedly replete, basked on the ramparts, regretful to be leaving that gentle, radiant countryside. Soon after we had driven down the road which coils steeply round the village, the sky turned grey as we were crossing a causse where even the earth seemed harsh and ugly; so, nostalgic for the river, we turned north at Sauzet on D.23.

It brought us to Luzech, which is built on a rocky peninsula, for here the Lot makes one of its characteristic loops. But this natural defence, which enabled the little town to withstand many sieges and to be captured only once, by Richard Coeur de Lion, has now been harnessed by the dam of a bleak and hideous hydroelectric power station.

So we hurried away, but instead of crossing the river and taking D.9 and N.111 to Cahors, which would have been the better way, we kept to the left bank because I wanted to show Charles a château where I had spent a happy day in 1938. Although it had not been occupied since the Revolution, the land was farmed by a delightful old man who lived in the stable block and entertained me to lunch on home-tinned thrushes, and then insisted on my tasting the wine from nine barrels in the enormous cellar. As I had not then learned to spit out the wine at a tasting I could only drive back to Cahors by exerting the maximum concentration.

My host had offered to sell me a fifty-year lease of the house and garden for fifty pounds, and during the intervening years I had often thought how much I should like to live there. So the contrast between what the château would have been like after my restoration and its actual condition was a sharp disillusion. The towers were not stone but gimcrack, leprous with yellow scabs where the plaster had fallen. Where the paved garden had been, which imagination had planted with an exuberance of old-fashioned roses, a few scruffy hens scratched among spinach gone to seed. And the old man who had made me welcome was dead.

By six o'clock we reached Cahors; tired, hot and thristy. Thunder was sulking above the town, snoring under a fusty blanket of heat. I left Charles drinking beer outside a café in the main street while I, who tend to become infuriatingly efficient when overtired, strode off to find us a room. I expected to be welcomed—even perhaps remembered, at the Hotel Ambassadeurs, where I had stayed for a fortnight before the war and eaten superbly on less than four pounds a week. But the receptionist, who admitted grudgingly that she had a room vacant, became even more grudging when I said we might like to take it by the week. Nettled, I asked to see Monsieur le Patron, and was told, sharply, that Madame la Patronne was out.

I decided to walk to another hotel instead of using the car which was foolish of me as it was farther than I expected and I had not allowed for the oppressive heat. They too did not seem keen on long term visitors, although had I been less disgruntled I might have realized that their reaction was due only to surprise that English tourists wanted to stay in Cahors, instead of only stopping for the night on their way to Spain where, at that time, the exchange was so much more favourable.

"Give me a drink, and then we'll get out of this bloody town!" I exploded when I had trudged back to Charles. I snatched up the map and stared at it in desperation. A name gleamed through the fog of gloom—a small fugitive gleam—no more than the glimmering of a hunch; a tiny flame that must be sheltered from any harsh wind of analysis which might blow it out. "We will go to St. Cirq-Lapopie," I said decisively.

"But *why?*" he protested. "If you don't want to stay here, let's go the the Château de Mercués. It's only eleven kilometres and this place you've suddenly chosen is at least thirty. We are both too tired and too hot to start exploring at this time of the evening. For goodness' sake try to be sensible!"

"I won't be sensible!" I said furiously, feeling it unfair to snarl at him; but what else could he expect from an overstrained camel which was trying to find an oasis?

The map showed me that there were several ways of reaching St. Cirq-Lapopie. Logic suggested that we should take the riverside road, N.662, on which there were at least two hotels where we could have dinner, or even change our minds and stay the night. But logic at that moment seemed detestable—a cold neon light in whose harsh glare my glimmer of hunch would be invisible.

After Arcambal, where we left the route national, the road, D.8, wound steeply upwards. Wide views began to unfold, and then suddenly faded as though grey transparencies were being lowered across a stage panorama. The thunder ceased to snore, and roared as it awoke under its grey blanket. It switched on magnificent lightning, switched it off again, and upset a vast bath of water that made it impossible to drive the car. With one great roar, but this time a roar of laughter, the thunder tore the cloud-curtains into shreds and left for us a rainbow in the sky.

We wound down the windows. Air sparkling with vitality washed over us. We jumped out of the car. We hugged each other. Bright water-drops showered down from a bush of honeysuckle as we climbed the bank to see even more of this stupendous view: mile after mile of distance, hill after hill. It only added to our freedom that there was not a village, nor even a cottage, in sight.

We were gay again, eager for adventure. What did it matter if there were no room for us, or even no dinner, when we came to St. Cirq-Lapopie? We would drive on until we found where we were going. We had seen the rainbow.

And so we came to our beautiful village, by the high road which had already revealed to us such lavish splendour that when it turned yet again and we saw the tiers of roofs, and then the serene loveliness of the ancient houses, we could not quite believe it was real. Enchanted, we let the car glide down the curves to the bridge over the Lot. Now we must look up to see the village. It seemed to grow out of the rock, five hundred feet above its guardian river.

"We shall stay here—we must," said Charles. "If there is not a room in the hotel we will find one in a cottage, and it won't matter in the least if there isn't a loo."

So we drove up the hill again, slowly because there was so much to look at, and turned down a steep little street which in a few yards brought us on to the only piece of level ground that exists in St. Cirq-Lapopie. As we were getting out of the car a man who had been sitting outside Aux Bonnes Choses walked purposefully toward us.

"I hope you don't mind me speaking to you like this," he said, embarrassed, "but I saw the G.B. on your car and so I knew you were English—strangers in a strange land and all that makes it a bit stuffy to wait for an introduction."

For a moment my heart sank. Had our rainbow led us to a 'Beauty Spot' swarming with English tourists? Perhaps he guessed what I was thinking for he said hastily, "You are the first English people I've seen since I came here. Wish you had come sooner as I don't speak much French. This is the last day of my holiday and I'm catching the night train. Just wanted to tell you that you'll be very happy here. Madame Rochet is a wonder-

133

ful woman—really wonderful. Nothing is too much trouble. I'm a bit of an invalid and she has looked after me like a mother." He looked a little anxious, as though we might think him too exuberant. Then he amended his statement. "Madame Rochet will look after you *better* than a mother."

The moment we saw her we were at home. She showed me her three bedrooms. Which did I prefer? It would be the work of a moment to prepare the one the Englishman was vacating. I chose the one with two windows, and she seized a broom and started to sweep the floor. Then she discarded it and sat down on the bed, smiling at me contentedly. "So fond have I become of our English guest—and then, tonight, arrive two more English! And what is so wonderful is that you and your husband are English and yet can speak French!"

Through the open window I could hear the Englishman talking volubly. "Doesn't he speak French?" I asked her.

"But not a word. He cannot even understand it. He drinks no wine with his meals! A hundred times I have told him that there is no necessity for economy, that my wine is free; but still he does not drink any! Will you please explain to him before he goes that when I pressed wine on him I was not trying to sell it to him? How could he think that I would serve a meal without including wine in the price of the menu!" She sighed. "Such a considerate man he is, so courteous—and yet he does not seem pleased with my food, for he gives most of it to the dog and the cats—even the hens gather round his table, pecking fragments of my truffle omelette!"

She looked at me searchingly and I hastened to put her doubts at rest. "My husband and I are both gourmets, and we know the wine of Cahors; the wine which Henri Quatre declared to be the most noble in all France, and whose vines never succumbed to the phylloxera...."

"So you understand our Vieux Cahors! I knew you

would be happy here the moment I saw you! Now I must go and make a last omelette for my Englishman, and pack the provisions for his journey. If he cannot eat anything that I give him he would starve, poor dear creature, rather than attempt the mediocre food which he would be served in a station buffet or on a train."

By the time she brought his omelette he was in the grip of train-fever. She patted him on ths shoulder. "Now you must be calm and not worry, or you will get another attack of indigestion. In one hour the train will go. I refuse to allow you to risk a chill by waiting needlessly on the draughty station."

Obediently he started to eat. "How kind she is: how thoughtful," he observed. "Sometimes she has almost killed me with kindness. You see, I came here to recuperate from an operation for the removal of my gall-bladder: no fats, no alcohol, is the régime. But here no one speaks anything but French." He said this as though it were an odd quirk in the inhabitants of a remote French village. "The first two days I drank a little wine with my dinner, but I suffered for it! 'No fats,' I say to her, rubbing my stomach to show that it is no fault of mine that I must be so rigid in my diet." He ventured another bite. "She thinks I am hungry! She brings me more *pâte*—and how delicious it is, although I have to give to the animals all but a fragment. When she sees I am not quite up to the mark, she thinks I need feeding up and makes still richer sauces. It would be unhygienic to allow the cats to lick the sauce off my plate, so I sop bread in it which they swallow with the relish that I should feel if it were not for my disability."

He seemed shy at having talked about his symptoms, so to change the subject I told him that Charles and I had come to the Lot to write a book. "So you like books!" he exclaimed enthusiastically. "I am a painter: watercolours. I come to France every year to paint: wonderful scenery. I must write down some names for you..."

He began to scribble on the back of an envelope. I prattled on. At intervals he smiled, firing off remarks apparently at random. "Wonderful walks here. Are you great walkers? Good, good. Oh dear, I hope the taxi won't be late! So kind everyone is here but no sense of time whatsoever. They can't understand why I like to get to the station at least an hour before the train is due. Gives one a chance to relax before the journey."

He kept patting his suitcase to make sure it was still waiting patiently beside him. Madame Rochet came out with a brown-paper parcel, which must have contained enough to give him a stomach ache for a week, and tied it with a string to the handle. He was now gazing in a torment of anxiety at his watch. "I'm afraid the taxi will never come in time! Perhaps I must avail myself of your generous offer to drive me to the station."

He said this when we could hear a car grinding up the hill, a car whose horn was sounding a fanfare. "Of course we will take you. But I think this must be your taxi now," I said soothingly.

"It's most kind of you to tell me my watch is fast. But I assure you it isn't...."

Then he saw the taxi and shot to his feet. "Good-bye, good-bye!" He shook us warmly by the hand. "I can't tell you how much I've enjoyed our conversation. So glad you are so fond of reading. Hope you've brought plenty of books with you. Nothing much to do in the evenings except read."

Impatient as he was for the taxi to start, he leant out of the window and shook our hands again, shouting, "Good-bye, good-bye! So glad to have met you. Most people don't bother to talk with anyone who can only lip-read—it's a bit of a nuisance being stone deaf."

Chapter Eighteen
TO ALL GOOD THINGS

Only the most myopic visitor could fail to recognize why St. Cirq-Lapopie has often been called the most beautiful village in France, but I might have seen it through the admiring eyes of a stranger instead of with insight unless Madame Rochet had decided that we belonged there. So, except for the interlude at St. Céré, the Aux Bonnes Choses was our home until the middle of September, when we had to return to England because Charles's mother, in her ninetieth year, had had a stroke.

Our other mentor was Georges Cabessut, whose fierce independence usually permitted him to recognize the existence of tourists only when he put on a cap blazoned GUIDE to conduct the coach-load which arrived for a brief hour twice a week on their way to Pech Merle and Roc Amadour. This robustly piratical character, who before he was taken prisoner by the Nazis had implemented many ingenious Maquis schemes to harass them, decided that we were his cousins and should be accepted as such.

Georges found it surprising that we could not help him to pinpoint our exact relationship, for he not only knew the history of his family since they had settled in Lapopie, a mere five centuries, but had detailed records of the previous two hundred years at Cabessut, now part of Cahors, when the English sap in his Tree had stemmed from a knight in the Plantagenet army. He told me, rather apologetically, that although he knew his ancestors had come to Cahors from the Pyrenees, the records prior to the twelfth century were fragmentary, but that in those mountains there were still some of our cousins with whom he could put me in touch.

137

The care he and Madame Rochet took of us is exemplified by our homecoming after one of our few disappointing meals. As that bar-sinister on the gastronomic escutcheon of the Lot has now changed hands I will not disclose its locale—but these are only too accurate notes made the same evening:

"...is a pretty village, and might be an ideal place for people with children who don't want to be worried by the thought of them falling over the cliff. (Must remember to mention the remarkably good manners of Lapopie children. Is this due to the fact that only the ones who accept kindly advice survive long enough to breed?"

"Hotel looks pleasant although geraniums outside need watering. Very healthy amaryllis lilies in pots on the bar, and owner fetches a jug of water when I tell him that the flowers I have been collecting would also like a drink.

"Dinner is deplorable, and this cannot just be an off-day as four other couples who are *en pension* plod through it without protest. Soup seems to be river-water, muddy, with a few shreds of carrot and a dash of grease. Fish, unidentifiable, is bones and blotting-paper, so give it to a pair of charming cats who have remarkable green eyes with black rims to the eyelids. Country sausage, so good at Lapopie, is here uneatable. Charles takes a bite and exclaims 'Bats' Dung!'" Luckily no one understands English. The *vin compris* is nearly undrinkable, but we swallow some of it to foil the waitress who is hovering near, convinced that we shall be driven to buy a bottle of something better. To show we can't be bullied will wait for coffee and *digestif* until we get home."

Madame Rochet greeted us like a Nanny who fears her children have bĕen eaten by bears, so I asked her if the hotel had telephoned to say that we would not be back to dinner.

She admitted that this had been done. "But it was

not you who spoke to me, so how could I warn you! Either you are starving or else you will suffer agonies in the night. The cook there is a pustule on the face of France; worse, she is a living insult to the cuisine of the Lot. I insist that you tell me in detail what she gave you!"

I touched lightly on the soup. Madame Rochet cast up her eyes in horror. I described the fish. "Oh! Those poor cats!" she cried, and then decided not to waste her sympathy. "Doubtless they are common cats, and such creatures survive even by scavenging from dustbins. Then what did she give you?"

"Something, that described itself on the menu as *Saucisson de compagne....*"

"Surely the good God warned you not to touch it!"

I reassurred her. I had been spared: Charles had eaten no more than a small mouthful, and his interior was robust.

"Describe the sausage," she demanded.

"To do it justice I must use his exact words, which he pronounced loudly and clearly so that all could hear." I paused, wondering whether it would be too dishonest not to admit he had spoken in English, and decided that my duty was to my audience.

"Tell me," she urged. "Tell me exactly what he said."

"He speared a fragment on his fork. He stared at it, as a scientist stares into his microscope. Then he announced his opinion. 'Never before have I been offered what appears to be *merde de chauve-souris!'*"

"*Merde de chauve-souris!* Ah, what an exquisitely discerning description of that slattern's cooking!"

Shouting with laughter she swept us into the kitchen where the table was piled high with lime branches which Georges was stripping to make lime-flower tea. "*Saucisse merde de chauve-souris* is what they were given," she exulted. Georges was equally delighted. Lapopie had scored a goal against the ungodly, and we were the umpires who had announced the victory.

139

Suddenly remembering the speed and range of the Lotoise grapevine I began to feel a little guilty. "It is unfair to judge a hotel by a single meal—and anyway I was trying to be funny. In England there are hundreds of hotels where they serve meals even more dreadful...."

"And why?" Madame Rochet thundered. "Why, even in France, is good food becoming each day more difficult to find? It is because people allow themselves to be bullied; to accept any filth they are given! Are we Germans that we permit little Hitlers to rule our kitchens?" She turned to Georges. "Is it not true I said that if they came back and told us they had had a passable dinner I should know they felt it necessary to lie to me—to me, Madame Rochet! And this would have made it very difficult neither to lose my temper nor to weep. Did I not say this, Georges?"

Georges beamed at us. "This is exactly what she said, not once but many times. And I told her that she gave herself needless anxiety."

To conceal her emotion Madame Rochet flung open the refrigerator and rummaged among its crowded shelves for a tin of her finest *pâté de fois gras*. Then she rushed into the dining-room and from the top shelf of the lovely walnut cupboard took down a cherished bottle of fifty-year-old Armagnac.

"There are only four bottles of this left," she said, stroking the one she held as though it were the cheek of a favourite grandchild. "I never sell even a glass, for it is too fine to be drunk except as a gift."

She poured libations into four glasses. "There are very few of us left," she said gently. "Tonight we four will share a little supper together, for when your work is to share your roof with strangers, it is a happy thing to find yourself at home among friends."

Chapter Nineteen
TERROR BY NIGHT

We had only been at St. Cirq-Lapopie for a week
when Charles was jarred awake by a scream, at three
o'clock in the morning. Two seconds later he heard it
again—one word, high-pitched, anguished, and two
separated syllables: *"All-ez!"*

He was sitting bolt upright when it came again. *"All-
ez!"* He switched on the light and ran to the window.
"All-ez!"—ripped the stillness for the fourth time. Was it
a child? A child in the toils of nightmare? No, too loud
for a child. Again the air vibrated with naked terror:
"All-ez...all-ez!"

The silence closed in again. The hairs on his forearm
stood up like hackles. He listened intently, leaning out
of the window: no voice, no running feet, no gleam of
light through the slats of shutters...nothing. Was a lunatic
shut in one of the silent houses, or had he heard murder?
He pulled on a shirt and trousers, turned off the light so
as to watch unseen. If he saw someone slinking away
through the shadows should he tell Madame Rochet to
telephone for the police before he gave chase? He
wondered why the screams hadn't woken me, and was
relieved for my sake that I was still asleep.

For an hour he stayed at the window, lighting one
cigarette from the stub of another. Then he went back
to bed. In the morning he told me. "I'm glad you didn't
hear it," he added. "It was very unpleasant. *Allez!*—six
times. The first scream woke me. I never knew a single
word could hold so much fear."

"I expect it was a spook. Otherwise I should have
heard it too," I said consolingly.

"Nonsense! I was wide awake. I even switched off the
light again so as not to be a conspicuous target as I
watched from the window."

Madame Rochet and Georges Cabessut

"You heard a spook scream when you were in the south of France—at the Villa St. Joseph, before you met me. There were eight people in the house but only four heard it. And you searched the garden for hours because you were so certain that you had heard a murder."

"And so I had," he said. "Only it took place fifty years earlier—as you described in great detail when you were psychometrizing my watch. But I am certain that whoever screamed *Allez* was entirely solid. The noise was too loud to have been made by a spook."

He clung to this theory even when Madame Rochet, who wakes at the slightest sound, and Georges, and Hugette—who lived next door and did our washing, and Hugette's grandmother, who, although she was over ninety, had such sharp ears that she heard everything almost before it happened, all assured him that they had heard nothing in the night."

"Monsieur Beatty has had a nightmare," they said, But they glanced at each other and said it too vehemently.

Each found a way to avoid the subject. Georges recounted to Charles how one of the village stalwarts had recently won a bet that he would lay the oldest, ugliest and most arid local spinster. He was in the process of so doing when his wife, a renowned virago, entered the arena and started to upbraid him. "But we men of Lapopie do not allow ourselves to be bullied," said Georges complacently. "So he carried on until the job was done, and then took off his belt and gave his wife a sound thrashing for being so immodest as to watch."

Hugette, instead of staying to gossip when she brought back our laundry, paused only long enough to gather up an armful of my clothes and then hurried away, assuring me they would look much nicer after she had pressed them. Even Madame Rochet was evasive and tried to make me move into one of the other rooms on the excuse that I might sleep more soundly in a different bed. When I assured her that I was sleeping better than I had done for months she still insisted on giving me another mattress.

Their over-solicitude was making us feel uneasy. Was the sound of the scream a recognized prelude to disaster? To take our minds off this unwelcome thought we decided to go for a drive; and to prove to myself that I was feeling thoroughly 'down-here' and efficient I took detailed notes, which I will include because thereafter I ceased to take any, except of names and prices which I find difficult to remember.

St. Cirq-Lapopie. 13th June 1956

After lunch take D.8 and D.52 to Esclauzel, Concots, and Limogne. Views even better than when coming along this road from the other direction. Must remember to stress that the Lot, for over 70 kilometres to the east of Cahors, has a road along both banks, and that from them the views are not only entirely different according to whether one is travelling from east or west, but are from different angles—up, from the water's edge, or down, from the cliffs.

At Limogne take N.111 towards Villefranche-de-Rouergue. See several people laughing uproariously by the roadside. Picnic party? Why here, on this dull main

143

road? Then notice little Simca straddled across a stone wall. Guardian angels must be kept even busier looking after French motorists than when acting as Nannies to Irish horsemen. Slow down and make 'can we help?' gestures. Simca survivors wave bottles, indicating 'Come and join the party', and point gaily to two motor bicycles, to show that they already have enough help. So wave back and drive on.

Villefranche-de-Rouergue is a pleasant old town, but quaintness of narrow streets seems artificial because hung with strings of paper flowers and tatty little pennants for tomorrow's fête. Was not in the right mood to appreciate the church of Notre Dame, or even to be particularly impressed by its two-hundred-foot tower which is poised above an enormous Gothic arch. The interior has some fine wood carvings but seemed cold and unmagical, perhaps because I am determined to keep out of range of spooks. Wander about until we come to a fairground. Caravans have rows of champagne bottles on their steps and among the geraniums of the window-boxes. Prizes for side-shows at fair, or do French gypsies drink champagne in quantity?

Come to a bridge over the Aveyron and see on the far side two very seedy hotels confronting each other whose names are an extreme overstatement, Grand hotel de l'Europe et de l'Univers, and Hotel du Globe. Decide that café-cognacs would revive us, so have them outside the Grand Hotel Moderne. Feel too lazy to ask whether I can look round it to check on its degree of modernity.

Charles starts worrying again about screams in the night. If their source was physical it is none of our business. But suppose it is a spook who urgently needs attention? Why didn't I hear it too if it was a spook?

Trying to deflect this train of thought I order an ice and when this ploy proves ineffective say soothingly that if it is a spook, and a spook which my superiors consider to be my business, no doubt it will turn up, probably when least expected. This seems cold comfort to Charles who says gloomily that he hopes I won't find it in the middle of dinner, and in public; as happened when I found myself sitting on the lap of a ghost in the Savoy Grill. Change this subject by saying I have just remembered that I promised to buy sweets for Monique, Hugette's child. Hurry off to get some before the shop closes. 8/— for three half-pound bags; twice the price of English ones, and they look rather stale. Hope she won't notice.

Both feel more cheerful on our way to Villeneuve d'Aveyron, by N.122. Then take D.48 to Ols-et-Rignodes— charming château in trees on right, and by D.86 to Ambeyrac where we keep to the left bank along the top of the escarpment. Soon see tower on our left and stop to explore it. Would tower, which still has the spiral stair intact, and the adjoining ruin, make an ideal house if restored and given some extra windows? Have almost planted the garden, using three great walnut trees which actually exist to shade imaginary terrace, when decide that site unsuitable, as grandchildren might stray across the road and fall over the precipice.

A little farther on we leave car again and walk to the edge of the cliffs which here make a loop that almost encloses a strip of cultivation nearly a mile wide. The fields below us are all sizes and shapes and each is a patch of pure colour. Pasture really does look like emerald velvet, in spite of this being a cliché, and fields of poppies look like sheets of scarlet silk. No sound except distant cow-bells. Wonderful textures in the valley as the light changes, and the reflection of poplar trees ripples in the silver-metal river.

Leave Charles happily brooking and wander off to collect flowers: campanulas, three varieties, Evening Primroses, Jacob's Ladder, and some whose name I don't remember, which are rather like foxgloves but have yellow flowers and narrower leaves. Come to a herd of cattle, sorrel red with enormous horns like the ones in Egyptian tomb paintings. Cattle in charge of a small boy who is standing on the edge of the cliff, waving his arms to stop them coming too close to it. Cattle ignore him and press forward, to turn aside only at the last moment. Boy quite unruffled at what seems to have been a narrow escape from being pushed over. Should hate to have the job of herding them. Boy starts whistling and shouts *"Allez!"* at the cattle, who obey by going to the pasture on the safe side of the road. Wish he had not shouted *"Allez!"*, but realize this is silly of me. Collect Charles who seems much more cheerful and is intent on the quality of the evening light in the valley instead of thinking about screams in the night. Realize that as the shadows of the poplars are so long it must be getting late, so instead of stopping for a drink at Cajarc we take the main road, on the right bank, home.

Charles mentioned the screaming again after we had gone to bed, but although I put a notebook handy in case either of us had a relevant dream, nothing happened and we both slept soundly.

I spent the morning doing flowers for the dining-room, because we were giving a lunch-party for Margot and Julien Pitt-Rivers who were bringing over Paddy Leigh-Fermor from their lovely Château du Roc at Fons. Madame Rochet excelled herself, and glowed at the compliments showered on her as she produced relays of delectable food. Asparagus, each stalk as thick as my thumb and green and succulent for all its length, followed the *pâte de fois gras.* There were sweetbreads with mushrooms in a subtle sauce before the admirable chickens. Then there was a perfection of salad, and by this time we were all so full that only greed drove us to tackle the strawberries.

It was a gay party, and nothing was further from my mind than spooks, when, about four-thirty, we rose from the table and decided that a stroll would be the best method of shaking down lunch. We were all feeling somnolent from over-eating, but we wandered about admiring the view and listening to Julien and Paddy making intelligent comments about architecture. If I was feeling anything as we walked up to the church it was a slight smugness that we had found Madame Rochet, while Margot and Julien who lived within forty miles of her had never even been to St. Cirq-Lapopie.

Abruptly I found my focus of attention beginning to shift, and knew I must be careful not to start talking with anyone they could not see in case this caused them to think they had lunched with a lunatic. I tried to tune out the other wavelength but it was too insistent. So I left them, hoping to return before my absence was noticed.

Within a couple of minutes I was climbing over a wall into an abandoned garden. The slope was steep and the turf very slippery, but though a facet of my mind was urging me to take care in case I slipped a disc again, it was as though someone was pushing me along with a hand in the small of my back. It was a benign directive, this I knew for certain, which was with me to make sure that I kept my balance—that I did not stumble when I ran along a narrow ledge which led to a stone bench for my body to sit on. Until later I did not notice that the 'bench' was in fact only a block of stone which must have been part of the outer wall before the castle was demolished, or that it was on a rocky outcrop, within a yard of a sheer drop of over three hundred feet.

All I knew was that I need go no farther because I had come to the place where I was needed. I could feel my heart thudding, and knew this was not due to the exertion of the climb but was only a familiar symptom of being conscious on two levels simultaneously. To check that my critical faculty was working I took my pulse: fast, but not too fast, about a hundred and twenty. Being now ready, I leaned forward and covered my eyes with my hands, so as to cut off sensory impressions and identify more clearly.

"From these heights have many men died."

Why bother to tell me this when I knew it already? Soldiers were thrown from these walls by other soldiers who stormed the castle, but the ghost I have come to free was not a soldier.

The scene changes. Now it is not soldiers who kill each other. Men are dying because of the rivalries of dogma. Eleven have been adjudged heretics, and churchmen have given them into the power of the executioner who has forty soldiers with him to see that the sentences are carried out. The prisoners are to die by falling from the cliff—a refinement of cruelty because this is the death imposed only on traitors to Lapopie.

The executioner is a dark, squat man, his face deeply pock-marked. He reads out eleven names. Each man in turn goes nobly to his death. One of them even whistles as he strolls to the edge. How can he whistle? Surely his mouth must be too dry with the foretaste of death? Another of them is even more gallant. He stands poised on the brink with his hands above his head and shouts to the crowd: "Now for a high dive before I go for a long swim in the river!"

The last victim is a boy of seventeen. It is he who inspired the others to revolt against dogma, but now his courage falters. He stares at the executioner and cries out: "I am not ready to die yet! Give me more time...more time! I have not finished my prayers...."

The executioner takes a pace forward. The crowd, huddled together, weeping, begins to pray aloud.

The executioner takes another pace forward. And, as though there were an iron bar between them, the boy involuntarily takes a pace back.

The boy's taut nerves wring a scream from his parched throat: *"All-ez! All-ez!"* But instead of halting, the executioner inexorably takes yet another pace forward.

The ground seems to crumble under the boy's feet. And the prayers of the people of Lapopie surge up into the air.

They find his body lying dead at the foot of the cliff. But not a bone of it is broken, and on the flesh there are no bruises. The face is serene, smiling. And the people whisper of a miracle.

148

The men who had seen this become men again instead of cattle. And that night they fought against those who had come to subdue them in the name of religion: and to the executioner they accorded the death he had inflicted.

Again a man is being driven over the cliff: but this victim is the executioner, who is not brave. He screams as he reads the eyes of the men and women of Lapopie who, in a narrowing semicircle, close in upon him, pace by pace. *"All-ez...All-ez...All-ez!"* His voice is shrill with terror, as though it were the voice of a woman or boy screaming for pity. But there is no pity for him; for he had been pitiless.

"Now has the time come for his ghost to be set free of his fear." I knew it was I who had spoken these words, involuntarily. I checked myself, and silently asked that I need go no further. And in silence heard the answer. "It is not for you to question. It is for you to feel, and to bring all you know of love into your feeling."

"No, I cannot. Why should this ghost go free? How can I feel compassion for that manner of a man?"

"He is in fear, and fear is the great enemy. Free him from the enemy in the name of love. Be brave in love, and take upon yourself his fear so that he may overcome it."

I tried to do so; but such a dreadful vertigo assailed me that I jerked my eyes open, thinking that it was I who was being driven backwards, pace by slow pace, to the cliff's edge.

To my intense relief I saw Charles. "We got here half a minute ago," he said, "but you were too far out to hear us. Don't worry about the others. I've explained about the screams I heard, and how I hoped you would be able to do something about it. They understand, so go ahead."

It was reassuring to know that they would look after my body for me. Margot was sitting beside me and Julien was lying on the ledge at my feet so that even if I toppled forward I could not fall over the cliff. I heard

149

Charles tell me he had a notebook with him, and then kept only sufficient contact to know that I was recording what I experienced, although my voice sounded to me as though the words were being spoken in the distance.

"Fear is the great enemy, but love is stronger than fear. Let this man's fear enter into me; so that in the strength of my heart, and in the love of my fellow-men, his fear which falls like a stone into the Dark River can become light as the wings of a swallow, blessed of Thy river and Thy air."

Having made my invocation, I was able to achieve that degree of identification which enabled me to speak directly to the man I had come to free. "I have come to tell you that there is no longer any cause for fear. Now you can see the glory of the high place, and know the cliff only as the home of swallows. You are no longer the man who fell; for you can rest on the air as though on a goosefeather bed. You have not fallen. You do not lie at the foot of the cliff. There is no fear in you, and no pain.

"Walk with me, and feel the moss under your feet. Come with me to the river, and I will give you water; and from the fields beyond the river I will give you grain to make your own bread. If there is still a stain of spilt blood upon you I will give you of my blood, fresh and clean to wash you. For I give you my love freely, so take it and go from here: free.

"Bless you in the name of the Gods; whose name is in the rocks and in the grass, and in the swallows; whose name is in the water and in the fire and in the sky. Bless you. But remember that, like all blessings, this cannot endure even for an instant unless it lives by the love in your own heart."

Chapter Twenty
EVENSONG

The following morning, a piercing shriek from Madame Rochet sent me hurtling to the kitchen, convinced I should find her bleeding or boiled or burned; for I had not yet learned that had she been feeling anguish, either mental or physical, she would have expressed it by extreme understatement. After admonishing me for risking a fall by running so fast down the stairs, she explained that she had only been rebuking Tyoo, Hugette's caricature of a beagle, for stealing an egg.

"Tyoo used to snatch the eggs from my poor hens almost before they were laid, but the new rooster is fierce and pecks him, so he has the audacity to creep in here and steal them from under my nose," she said indignantly, while pouring for me a restorative cup of coffee. "I do not mind a dog being greedy, nor a dog who pretends to soft-hearted visitors that he is starving when in fact he has already stuffed himself until he can hardly swallow...."

She paused, and I knew this was my cue to confess that for our first few days we too had been deceived by Tyoo. "He put on such a pathetic expression that we were bullied into sharing our meals with him. But we thought we did it so discreetly that you hadn't noticed!"

She was swept by a gale of laughter. "That was very generous of you...if not very discerning. How could I fail to know what you were doing when there was grease on the floor after every meal—even more of it than when the poor-dear-artist-with-a-weak-stomach-who-was-deaf sat at the same table. Now you understand why I call it my *table des Anglais*. But drink your coffee in peace for this morning we shall not again be disturbed by Tyoo, who has stolen his sixth egg. One must admit that Tyoo is an intelligent dog and not merely a good actor—most people cannot stop acting, but not every dog can count up to six. Always six eggs he steals, and one by one he carries them to his picnic place in the site of the castle, and only when all six are collected does he start to eat them."

She went to the door and shouted, "Hugette!! *Pique-nique!!*" Then after picking up a knife, she started to prepare *haricots verts* while explaining that Hugette would now go to Tyoo's picnic place in time to rescue the eggs unbroken. Hugette would then scold him, put on his collar, and chain him to the letter-box beside her front door. "But of course she gives him a rug to sit on, and it is not too severe a punishment for he knows it will only last for half an hour."

At this point Charles came into the kitchen, and we helped her with the beans until she suddenly leapt to her feet, exclaiming: "We shall be late at the Dauras."

Without giving us time to tidy ourselves she swept us down the narrow street, which leads from the back-door at an angle more suitable for toboggans, talking so fast that we gathered only that she loved the Dauras who would therefore love us; that they had returned home from America late last night; and that they were people of acute perception who would be delighted to receive us at eleven o'clock in the morning.

We arrived precipitately at the house which Georges had pointed out as being one of the glories of Lapopie, "built in the thirteenth century as a hospital under the care of the bishops of Cahors". Madame Rochet banged on the door, and after warmly embracing the woman who opened it announced, "Here are two friends who are impatient to meet you!" and then left us.

In spite of finding two total strangers, embarrassed and dishevelled on her doorstep, Louise Daura and her husband, Pierre, accepted us as serenely on that first morning as they did on so many other mornings when

Louise and Pierre Daura in their 13th century home

we came, on the pretence of working, to the studio they lent us at the top of their garden. They had found Lapopie in 1926 and bought the house which gradually they had restored until it seems unchanged by the passing of half a dozen centuries. The studio had been the house of a seventeenth-century guild worker, which Pierre had rescued from demolition by transporting it to Lapopie stone by stone. No two people could have been more congruous in that setting, for Pierre is not only a fine artist and sculptor but looks as though he might have been the medieval model of a saint for Chartres Cathedral, and Louise radiates the same calm wisdom, lively with affectionate insight.

We had only known each other a few days when Louise heard on the grapevine, which is usually more reliable than Lotoise telephones, that an ancient château of outstanding beauty, with its entire contents of objects even more outstandingly beautiful, was for sale. "The grapevine is rather vague about the exact locality but I gather it is not far from Vers," said Louise, "and the name is something like Girondelle."

After scrutinizing the map we found Gironde, in the smallest type, close to the rectangle which indicates a minor château, so the three of us set out to look for it; Pierre, although interested in our envisaged treasures, having refused to be seduced from his painting. We took the main Cahors road, N.662, until Vers and then branched off on D.49 to Cours. Here I directed operations along a track which became increasingly narrow until it petered out in a huddle of derelict cottages, perched on the brink of a steep valley.

"No road: no château," said Charles briskly.

In spite of the evidence I still believed I was on the beam, so before he could turn the car I hopped out and approached an old woman who was staring suspiciously at us across a dung-heap. At first she pretended to be deaf, and seemed as ill-tempered as her two wolfish dogs which circled round me snarling. "The Château de Gironde? It is for sale? It is near here?"

Suddenly her wrinkled lips cracked open with a smile, showing a solitary tooth, white as the kernel of a fresh walnut. So we had come to visit the château? We must forgive her the stupidity of not instantly recognizing that we were friends. She had mistaken us for strangers. We would be most welcome. Perhaps it would be easier to leave the car in her care as the road was not quite suitable for so large a vehicle.

She conducted us to the gap between two barns and pointed to the path we must follow, which led through steep and stony fields. It soon became steeper, among stunted oaks. Slippery slabs of rock alternated with patches of loose stones which turned underfoot and rolled clattering down the hillside. We climbed two dry-stone walls, the first treacherous with strands of rotting barbed wire, the second lively with lizards.

Then there was a sudden blaze of scarlet ahead of us: poppies that almost hid the sparse blades of corn in a narrow field. A little farther on there was another field, with a thick crop of potatoes growing feebly in the stony ground. The stunted oaks closed in again as the path widened enough for us no longer to have to walk in single file. Abruptly we came to an open space of turf, purple with thyme, its scent pungent in the hot sunlight. Beyond the purple sward were the grey stone walls, the rust-red pantiles of a derelict building. Had it ever been a château? Perhaps, for there was a round tower, traces of walls which had once enclosed a courtyard, an imperishable elegance in the setting of the windows.

Something moved in the shadow of a grapevine which sprawled among the boughs of an ancient plum-tree. An old woman hobbled painfully into the sunlight, using a forked branch as a crutch. She called out an eager welcome. Her wispy white hair hung loose to her bowed shoulders and her black clothes were held together with twine and safety-pins. Why was she so pleased to see us? Who did she think we were?

"I knew you would come soon," she said. "I kept telling him you would come soon."

Louise tried to explain, to apologize for our intrusion, but she did not listen. "You must not mind my taking you into the kitchen," she said, beckoning us to follow her. "You must forgive everything here being a little untidy. If I had known you were coming today I would have opened the shutters, prepared a meal for you."

The walls and ceiling of the kitchen were blackened with smoke from the huge fireplace, and so little daylight filtered through the broken slats that for a moment I did not see the old man sitting in a high-backed walnut chair by the hearth. He tried to get up, but she gently forbade him, assuring him that we would forgive his apparent discourtesy. "His heart is very weak," she whispered to me. "He must not exert himself."

Her husband bowed to each of us in turn and asked us to be seated. I saw there was only one other chair in the room, a small, rush-seated chair that had one of its legs mended with copper wire; and that the only other furniture was a massive refectory table, two wooden stools and a grandfather clock. But I knew that this was not the hospitality he offered; it belonged to an earlier setting, where fine woods wore the sheen of beeswax and silk damask from Lyon folded against bright walls. His eyes were calm and clear as his voice, blue as the veins on his long sensitive hands, hands born to guide a pen or a rapier instead of a plough. His wife, seeing that he was happy talking to Charles, beckoned to Louise and me to follow her into the adjoining room. "He does not like to concern himself with business," she said. "It is we who will discuss the sale."

"I'm afraid we have not come to buy the house," said Louise humbly.

She brushed this aside. "It is too soon to speak of money matters. I wish to show you my beautiful things."

She hobbled eagerly from room to room, six large rooms of fine proportions whose walls still bore traces of eighteenth-century gilding. In each there was an enormous cupboard, fourteen or more feet high, the panels carved deep into planks of solid walnut. Each room had a walnut bed, a *lit de bateau*, one sheltered by curtains hung from the ceiling, of silk so tattered that the original rose colour was grey as the cobwebs which festooned them. From each bed she stripped off the worn covers so that we could see the plumpness of the feather mattress she had made from geese of her own plucking. "I cannot sleep in a good bed any longer," she said regretfully. "A soft bed makes my back hurt too much, so I spend the night in my little chair by the hearth."

"A board under the mattress would help," I said. "It is better for your back to be straight when it is painful."

"How do you know?"

"Because after I hurt my back I used to sleep on a mattress on the floor. All last winter I slept like that...."

"You hurt your back as I did, and yet you walk without a stick? You walked from the road? That is good news! I wish you had been here to tell the doctors in Cahors that they were fools when they said I would never recover from my fall last autumn. She patted me on the shoulder. "I have the rheumatism. Rheumatism? It is nothing! Everyone has the rheumatism. All doctors are fools. Three years ago, after my husband had the great bleeding from his stomach and they cut him open in the hospital at Cahors, they said he could not live more than three months. Three years ago they told me that, because they would not believe that I could look after him so well. Of course I can look after him! I am much younger, much stronger than he is. He, though you would not believe it, was eighty-six years old last February; and I shall be only eighty-one next May. Now I shall sleep like you did on hard boards and soon throw away this stupid stick. Where shall I find boards? Of course! The shelves of my linen press!"

We helped her to arrange the bed. The shelves were so heavy that we could only just lift them. She lay down for a moment and insisted that for the first time for many days she was free from pain. I wished I could have believed that the nagging ache would not return as soon as there was nothing to deflect her attention from it.

If only there had been something to buy that was small enough to carry away; but it would have taken an ox-cart to transport the least massive piece of her remaining furniture. And there was no road for the ox-cart. She must have felt our embarrassment. "You must blame my stupid eyesight for mistaking you for the people who had come to buy," she said gently. "I am doubly fortunate that they did not come today for they would have kept me bargaining when I wished to be free to entertain you."

She opened a cupboard and brought out a dusty, half-empty bottle of ratafia, and three glasses. I think it was her last, but it would have been an unforgiveable insult to refuse it or to offer to pay.

"They will come tomorrow," she said again, after she had taken a glass to Charles. "They, the people who will buy the house and the furniture, have not let us know when they are coming so we do not yet know who they will be. But of course they will come soon, for it is over a month since a friend from the village put an advertisement about the château in the newspaper."

She insisted on refilling our glasses. "You must come to visit us when we are living in Cahors. With the money from the sale of this fine property we shall buy a small house which will be very easy for me to look after. It will no longer matter that I cannot dig the garden as well as I used to do, or that I am not so quick now at chopping wood for the fire. Always there must be a fire, even in summer, for my husband feels the cold, now that he cannot move very much. When I want vegetables I shall buy them in the market, and I shall buy wine there too. And my husband will have people of his own kind to talk to, educated people." For a moment she looked sad. Then she said confidently, "But he will always need me to look after him. He has always needed me."

She stood in the doorway of the house that had no road leading to it, waving to us as we went away. She was sure that tomorrow or the next day a buyer would come, as a child is sure of the coming of Santa Claus.

Chapter Twenty-one
ON SNAILS AND SERPENTS

Most of my travel memories have to go through a fine-meshed sieve before I really enjoy reliving them. The sieve removes midges from trout streams, black palls of flies from Highland moors, fleas from the Iraqi desert and mosquitoes from almost everywhere which is not too cold for comfort. But the Lot needs no sieve, for such sources of discomfort are minimal. Cherry-trees, peach-trees, plum-trees in their season are heavy with fruit; yet I never saw a wasp. Two hornets appeared one day during luncheon at Aux Bonnes Choses, but did no more than blunder about the room and so give a young visitor from Paris an excuse to stand on a chair and show off her pretty legs. The only mosquitoes I met would have been easy to eliminate, for they were breeding in an ornamental pool at the Château de Mercuès where we were strolling in the garden after an excellent dinner. We suffered only from three fleas. The first had strayed from one of Madame Rochet's hens which took refuge under our bed after being startled by a visiting dog. The other two sprang on us from their sanctuary in the soutane of a venerable abbé; so agile and voracious a brace that we hunted them during three nights of mounting frustration until Charles finally trapped them on a piece of damp soap.

I had expected, and feared, to find quantities of snakes, for Freda White,* who is much braver than I am, recommends throwing small pebbles at vipers which are sunning themselves on the path should the adjacent ground be too precipitous to scramble past

* *Three Rivers of France,* Faber and Faber, 1952.

them. Edward Harrison, in his enchanting *Two Summers in Guyenne*, the summers of 1892 and '93, makes some even more alarming comments, although he is here referring to the upper reaches of the Dordogne: "Snakes rustled as I passed and hid themselves among the stones. To my mind they were much more to be dreaded than the wild boars, for these stony solitudes swarm with adders, of which the most venomous kind is the red viper, or *aspic*. Its bite has often proved mortal."

However, when this robust character had narrowly avoided stepping on an *aspic*, which he recognized by its olive skin with reddish patches, he reluctantly considered it to be his duty to kill it, and felt guilty for doing so because, "After being roused by a blow the creature did not attempt to run, but did battle bravely, fiercely striking at the stick."

Charles told me we had run over several snakes, but being intent on the map or the view I did not see any of them until he suddenly slammed on the brakes and jumped out of the car exclaiming, "There is a remarkably long snake in the road!"

While he ran eagerly towards it I prayed that it was thoroughly dead. Fortunately it was, and what at first sight had seemed to be seven feet of serpent was in fact two snakes which had been run over while trying to swallow the same rat.

The only time I encountered a live viper was on the causse above Lapopie where I was collecting flowers. I was not even expecting to see one, for the short, springy turf provided no cover except a few stunted juniper bushes. I was squatting down beside one of these when it suddenly exploded into activity. A larger viper, lashing its coils, was glaring into my horrified eyes from a range of eighteen inches. I thought it was trying to struggle free from the thorns only so that it could hurl itself at me.

"You could not have yelled louder if it had bitten your behind," said Charles, unsympathetic after running so hard in response to my frenzied shriek. Trying to look dignified—which is difficult when one's legs are shaking with panic—I stalked to the car and hurried into it.

I no longer wished to collect flowers, for this might involve meeting more snakes; but it was a Saturday evening and I cherished the honour of being called Madame la Floriste by the gastronomes who thought nothing of driving a hundred miles in homage to Madame Rochet's Sunday lunch. Luckily, on the road down to St. Gery, I saw quantities of a variety of scabious I had not seen before—nor since. On stalks like a black wire a metre or more in length, their coronal of white petals surrounded a jet-black thimble which, when in bud, resembled a conical cushion of vivid green pins. But what made them an even greater delight was that they grew on the verges, so I could gather them without leaving the tarmac. But to reach the bushes of honeysuckle, glistening with scarlet berries, I should have to clamber down a bank where rocky ledge offered ideal sunbathing places for somnolent serpents....

Perhaps if I walked purposefully towards a perilously steep place....

"If you want honeysuckle, why not ask me to get it for you?" said Charles. "If you insist on trying to climb down there you're almost certain to rick your back."

So I got obediently back into the car—and both of us were happy.

On our way home we saw a small Citroën, driven by a middleaged woman, draw up exactly opposite the snake-place. Charles thought the car had broken down, and as the woman was alone he stopped to offer assistance. She assured him that the car marched perfectly and that she had paused for a moment only to admire the view. As she had chosen about the only place on that road, D.8, where views are minimal, it would have been tactful to accept her excuse and leave her to carry out her real intention. But I felt this was not the moment for tact. "Madame!" I exclaimed, "I beseech you! Not there! In that bush lives a most formidable serpent!"

She gasped, blushed, slammed the door of the car and drove away so fast that she nearly left the road at the next corner. "You meant well," said Charles, "but she seems to have been startled by such kindly advice by the allegedly inhibited English."

An hour or two later I was walking to the edge of the cliff to throw away an armful of dead flowers when I met Louise, so I told her about the viper. "When I was a girl I was bitten by a Cottonmouth Moccasin," she said in her soft slow voice." Cottonmouth Moccasins are very, very poisonous."

"Did it kill you?" I exclaimed.

"No," said Louise, "It did not kill me, but it made me very ill."

"How did it happen? When? Where?"

"It happened when I was a little girl of ten years old, when I was with my mother in a summer cabin we had in the Alleghany Mountains. I had been down to the swimming-hole by myself, and on the way back to the cabin I was crossing a rickety little bridge over a stream. My bare foot slipped down between two rotten planks and I felt something stick into the side of my foot. I thought I had trodden on a rusty nail, until I tried to pull my foot free and could not move it. So I bent down and looked over the edge of the bridge, expecting to see a thorn-bush which had drifted down and got wedged under the planks. But it was not a thorn-bush; it was a very, very big Cottonmouth Moccasin, which had its fangs stuck right into the side of my bare foot. So then I let out a yell, and somehow I managed to tear my foot free. Then I ran up the path to the cabin, shrieking for my mother...." Louise sounded apologetic for having yelled, but even hearing about it made me almost speechless with horror.

"What did your mother do?"

"Oh, Mother is a very calm woman. She sucked out the poison from my foot, and then she washed out her mouth with Listerine, and then she telephoned the doctor. The doctor gave me a serum injection but I was very sorry for myself for several days. When I was well again my mother told me that she was so scared when she knew I had been bitten by a Cottonmouth Moccasin that she nearly fainted; and that if she had fainted I would amost certainly have died."

That same evening I found Louise standing on a stool while she tried to reach a snail that was clinging to the ceiling of her kitchen. Then I saw that there were snails on the walls, snails on the table, snails inching their way purposefully across the floor.

"Goodness how tiresome," I said feelingly, "even when we lived in Cornwall and snails ate everything in the garden at least they did not chase us indoors."

"A friend brought them as a present for Pierre, but we were out, so she put them on the window-sill and they escaped from their bag," said Louise placidly, as I managed to steady the stool just before it toppled.

I was glad to be able to help her, having become an efficient snail handler through caring for Eustace, whom I had found cowering in a lettuce when I lived in Albany, that cloister off Piccadilly where the more usual pets are not allowed. He had grown from the size of my little finger-nail to a full four inches when extended, and rode contentedly on my shoulder when I took him for an outing to St. James's Park.

Louise captured the last snail and put it with the rest of the four dozen in a wire salad-basket, which she covered with a plate and hung from a hook in one of the rafters. She looked up at them sympathetically. "Poor things, they will have to stay in there and starve for ten days at least; preferably for a fortnight. I always hope they do not notice me preparing salads right under their prison."

"But I thought only Roman snails, the kind you get in restaurants, were edible."

"All snails are edible so far as I know. They can be grey or brown or blond or brindled. According to Pierre, the small ones that are striped like old-fashioned peppermint humbugs, called *Escargots des Vignes*, have an even better flavour than the *Petit Gris.*" She sighed. "I wish I enjoyed eating them, for then perhaps I shouldn't so much dislike preparing them."

I was shocked to think what quantities of free munch had escaped my attention during our two years in Cornwall, when the snail population had increased immoderately because the birds who were their natural opponents had been eaten by hawks and buzzards, whom myxomatosis had deprived of their normal diet of rabbits.

At first, fond memories of Eustace had caused me to pick his kinsmen gently off lettuces and carry them in a basket to distant pastures; but after they had finished off the vegetables and started to strip every leaf from the rose-bushes, acute animosity was the only emotion I felt as I stamped on them or threw them into a bucket of brine. Had I only known better I could have given banquets of snails instead of growing exasperated....

"Are they difficult to cook?" I asked Louise.

"Horrid rather than difficult. After they have starved, which empties the gut of anything poisonous they may have been eating, you put them in a bucket and sprinkle them with rough salt. This makes them disgorge their slime, and after about four hours you wash the slime off. This would be fairly easy if I could hold them under a running tap, but our well is so low that I have to wash them in a basin, which is a nastier job than laundering the handkerchiefs of a family who are all suffering from severe head-colds."

The image of myself as a *Chef d'Escargots* began to fade, but I was still curious to hear the rest of the process.

"Simmer them for an hour, and then take them out of the shells and wash them a lot more," said Louise. "Either rub each one in your hands or in a cloth, for this dislodges the black bit at the end of the body—which the French realistically call the *boule de merde*. This expertise was taught to me by the proprietress of the restaurant A l'Escargot in Figeac who is widely famed for her snails; she says it allows her customers to eat double their usual quantity without suffering even a twinge of indigestion. Then you wash the shells, if you are going to serve the snails in them, but in the Lot this is only done to please foreigners."

"We went to A l'Escargot in Figeac last week—Charles ate three dozen snails and said they were the best he had ever tasted, but several other customers were eating their snails out of shells and they all seemed to be French."

"By foreign I only meant French who are not also Lotoise. But I still have not told you how to cook snails. The next stage is to simmer them for two hours—without their shells of course—in a *court bouillon*. I make mine with three parts of water to one part of white wine, a dash of wine vinegar, the juice of a lemon, a shred of orange peel and a bouquet of herbs, preferably parsley, thyme, tarragon, fennel and a bay-leaf. Then all you have to do is to make some garlic butter to which you add plenty of chopped parsley, put each snail back into a shell and pour the butter over it and then heat them piping hot in the oven when you want to eat them."

"For the first time I am glad to be allergic to garlic, for this gets me out of eating snails," I said fervently.

"That allergy won't provide an excuse in the Lot, for they have several non-garlic recipes. The washing and the simmering is always the same, but after that you can sauté them in butter and sprinkle them with parsley. Or you can eat them hot from the *court bouillon* and dunk them in iced mayonnaise. Or serve them with Sauce Americaine—which you can get from any cookery book giving this recipe for lobster. Or in a sauce made by sautéing small cubes of raw ham and chopped sorrel in butter and thickening it with a sprinkling of flour and some cream. If you can't get sorrel you can make do with spinach and a dash of lemon juice."

She looked sympathetically up at the salad basket through which the week-after-next's gastronomic treat was eyeing us reproachfully. One of them reminded me of Eustace. So I told Louise that Charles was waiting for me, for she does not use alcohol and I felt in need of a restorative drink.

Chapter Twenty-two
IN RESPECT OF RIVERS

At Conduché, where the main road tunnels through the cliff as it approaches St. Cirq-Lapopie, another lovely river, the Célé, flows through a narrower, wilder gorge to join the Lot. The first village upstream is Cabrerets, with a little hotel, Les Grottes, where we often went to enjoy a carafe of wine in the coolness of the garden, or for a meal surpassed only by Madame Rochet's. The garden is, in the most literal sense, a summer-house, roofed with grapevines from which the bunches hung like light fittings, and divided by walls of runner-beans and morning-glories growing up strings, into glaucous, rustling rooms; in one of them two huge pet carp drowsed in a sunken bath, curving about each other like sleek dachshunds in a basket. Below it the river widens to a pool, where an ancient angler, somnolent as the carp, moved in his boat only to cast bread on the water or to gather a foolish fishlet from his float. The cliff beyond looks sheer, but there is a path which towards sunset becomes a processional of goats led by a little goatherd, evoking panpipes for this Attic frieze....

But even in 1956 such pleasing fantasies were sometimes interrupted by a turbulence of tourists, refreshing themselves after a visit to the Grotte du Pech Merle or the prehistoric museum which, through the devoted scholarship of the Abbé Lemozi, is housed in the fourteenth-century château that commands the village.

Pech Merle is now impressively equipped to receive visitors, but when I first descended into its depths, in the early spring of 1938, I found the experience disquieting. I had stopped in Caberets to ask the way to the cave and at first thought myself fortunate to have by chance addressed myself to the guide. Surely he must be the guide, for he had shambled off down an alley between two cottages and come running back clutching the key.

It was the right key, for it unlocked a narrow rust-stained door at the foot of a steep flight of steps which penetrated the bare hillside. Inside the door was an electric light switch, which he at first seemed reluctant to touch and then turned on only after taking a stub of candle from his trouser pocket and casting it over his shoulder.

After this declaration of faith in the lighting system he marched resolutely into the obfusc provided by a few dimly glowing bulbs which seemed very haphazardly attached to the dripping walls. When I realized that we were to explore not a single cave, however large, but a vast labyrinth, I wished that when in search of painted bulls I had had the wit of Ariadne who, when rash enough to seek the Minotaur, had at least provided herself with a thread to follow on her way out.

However, retreat was impracticable, because the current was insufficient for more than one stage of our journey to be illuminated at a time, and while there was at least a dim light ahead there was stygian darkness behind me. I felt increasingly uneasy when he let the darkness flood back for longer and longer intervals between turning off one series of lights and turning on the next. But still managed to pay some attention to the paintings, of mammoths and bulls and deer, until he suddenly became engulfed by a hurricane of laughter. The sound bounced from stalagmite to stalactite until it seemed we were ants imprisoned in a drum. Gradually the maniac mirth subsided into giggling: words bubbled through, sibilant, lisping; words which at last conveyed the joke he thought so terribly funny.

He had never been in the caves before, because everyone thought he would damage the paintings. But he had proved that he was more clever than anyone in the village, for he had stolen the keys from the guide's cottage, and now he was conducting the very first tourist of the season...and the very first tourist was sure to give him an enormous tip..."*Un pourboire énorme,*" he repeated truculently. And further to point the hint he turned out the lights.

The instinct for self-preservation alerted my wits. I promised to give him a *pourboire formidable,* but could do so only if we turned back to the car in which I had carelessly left all my money. We must hurry...hurry! For if we delayed my bag might be stolen...perhaps at this very minute it was being taken...leaving me powerless to reward him!

It worked. But so effectively that I had to run to keep up with him, down slimly steps, along narrow catwalks, ducking under stalactites, terrified that I might get left behind and reach the door to find it shut behind him. Fortunately he was too impatient to think of shutting the door, and as I reached the top of the entrance steps I saw him glowering down the road for a sight of the imaginary thief who was coming to steal his well-earned tip.

He was fulsome with gratitude when I left him, sitting on the bank admiring the pictures on the notes like a child playing with picture postcards. He looked pitifully huge and helpless in the sunlight. Yet I still wonder if he would have left me to die in the dark if he had realized that my note-case had not been in the car but in my pocket!

The Célé winds on among exclamations of poplars, between cliffs the colour of ripe quince and ripening apricot. The ridge to the south rises to a thousand feet, and so lovely are the views from each of the six roads that, between Cabrerets and Espagnac, climb over the crest to villages on the Lot, that I have never been able to decide which I shall first choose when I return there.

But I know my favourite village of the Célé valley is

Marcilhac, built within the confines of a tenth-century monastery, where there is a roofless and magical abbey church—burned by Huguenots in 1569, which I found when setting out after luncheon at the smaller hotel to look for a place at which to bathe. The river was too shallow for bathing, but lower down there are falls where I have lain tranquilly in a niche among boulders with my head dry and in the sun and water gushing over my shoulders.

Charles, who is a robust swimmer, preferred bathing in the Lot, which I also enjoyed except when the current was running too swiftly. Usually the water is olive-green and silk-soft to the skin, but after a summer storm has washed red-oche down some of the mountain streams of the upper reaches it surges along like a torrent of molten copper. The recognized bathing place is from a gravel bank by the bridge which links Lapopie with Tour-de-Faure, but we preferred a sandspit opposite the great crag on which the castle used to stand—although sand is an euphemism for it was dried mud mixed with fine gravel—because we could count on having it to ourselves, the only access to it being across a tobacco field belonging to a friend of Georges and along a secret path we had laboriously cut through a forest of nettles.

Charles went there one evening alone, and was annoyed to see someone's clothes lying at the edge of the water. So, hoping that the intruder would finish his bathe and depart, he took a turn or two along the aisle of poplars which is separated from the river by a heavily overgrown bank. When after a few minutes no one came up our private path he was at first impatient and then began to feel anxious. He hurried back and looked more closely at the clothes, which consisted of a pair of men's shorts, neatly folded, and a pair of canvas shoes. At first he thought that someone had camped there for the night and been careless enough to leave them behind. It was then that he noticed the footprints, a single line clearly defined, for ours had been washed away during the night by a storm: footprints going down into the river, but none coming out of it again.

The current was flowing too strongly for anyone to swim upstream, and if he had waded through the shallows he would have turned back when he came in sight of the weir. To the west Charles could see nearly half a mile of river before it turned again in obedience to the cliffs. The sun was low in the sky and part of the river was already in shadow, but there was plenty of light to show the head of a swimmer, had there been a swimmer to see. He told himself that the man had got out farther down and walked home in his bathing trunks, far too annoyed to bother to come back and retrieve his shorts. It was a probable story, but he didn't believe it. For one thing the banks were too steep for any one to pull himself out unless he were exceptionally strong, or lucky. Charles knew this, for he had tried to do it himself. Somewhere in the bushes which hid the edge of the water a man might be clinging to a root or an overhanging branch, too exhausted even to shout. So Charles swam across to the opposite side of the river, and then let himself be carried by the current until he was beyond the part of the bank where the bushes grow to which a man could cling. Then he forged his way across to more gentle water, and swam against it until he got back to the place where the stranger had entered the river.

Next morning the shorts were still there. We could see them far below us as we stood on the edge of the Lapopie cliff. Georges, who the night before had at last persuaded us that there was no point whatever in informing the police, still held to his opinion that the owner would soon retrieve them. At ten, at eleven, at noon, we again climbed to the crag; and each time reported to Georges that they were still there.

After lunch he began to get interested and said he

170

would come down to the river with us. He looked carefully at the single line of footprints, which had been meticulously preserved through being hardened by the morning sun, and agreed that no one else had been there except Charles, whose tracks were easily identifiable as he had kicked off his espadrilles as soon as he was clear of the nettles, and so left an imprint of bare feet. "The stranger," said Georges, "was a man with a big stomach." He had been examining the shorts and the canvas shoes. "If he had been a man tall enough to justify the size of this waistband he could not possibly have had such small feet. He is a rich man and a foreigner...."

"How do you know?" asked Charles.

"Because these shorts are not the kind that Frenchmen wear. And fat Frenchmen who wish to bathe go to such places as Biarritz, where they lie among other fat men, like porpoises stranded on a beach. And who but a *rich* fat man would have such tender feet that he walks in his shoes right into the water, and only when it is deep enough to support his fatness does he take them off and throw them here?"

He turned triumphantly to Charles. "That was a clue you did not notice. The shorts were neatly folded, but the shoes were not placed side by side. There is nothing in the pockets, not even a handerchief. He is a man so frightened of thieves that he puts his handkerchief as well as his money and his watch in a waterproof bag. Then he straps it round what serves him for a waist before he goes in swimming. This alone proves him a stranger to the Lot!"

Georges was still holding the shorts, and his description of their owner was so decisive that I thought he might be doing psychometry. And why not? He could find caves by dowsing, so why not psychometry from the buckle of a pair of shorts? He stared intently at the river and began talking to himself. "He is fat. He does not swim well. He is a stranger who does not know our rivers. He thinks the river is shallow all the way across and does not realize that a few strokes will take him out of his depth into the current...."

He turned to us and said with authority. "Please be very quiet and do not move. And it would be better if you would sit a little further away while I am working. If there is a dead body in the river it will be quite near us. I know the deep places and the currents. It will not float until tomorrow but I have my own way of finding a corpse...."

For about ten minutes he crouched motionless on his heels at the water's edge. Then he picked up a small stone and sent it curvetting over the surface of the river. Circles spread out, and he stared at them fixedly. Was he employing a technique similar to the one used by those who see in a crystal? A second stone spread ripples over an area downstream of the one covered by the first circles. His gaze was so intent that I thought he might go into a trance and fall forward into the water. I too stared at the circles until I felt dizzy. I began to slip back into myself as a child of nine when, early on a summer morning, alone on the Hayling Island beach, I had waded out to see what my Labrador had discovered in the shallows. It was the body of a drowned sailor. I knew the body belonged to a sailor because there was an anchor tattooed on the bloated chest. The chest seemed to be breathing under a kind of veil, until I saw that the veil was a cloud of nibbling shrimps.

So vivid was my imagination that I expected to see the face of the drowned stranger float slowly up to the surface, offering itself relentlessly to my gaze like some monstrous jelly-fish. Could I withdraw before they dragged the corpse to the bank?

Slowly Georges got to his feet. "There is no corpse here," he said. "The little fish would not have been attracted to the stones I threw if there had been a corpse here: they would have been too busy feeding on it."

No one ever solved the Great Shorts Mystery. Georges

showed them to all his friends. In every café for miles they were discussed. In the end Georges made up his mind, in spite of all our denials, that Charles had put them there himself, as an extraordinarily funny, if obscure, example of English humour.

The church at St-Cirq-Lapopie

Chapter Twenty-three
CANNIBALS AND CASTLES

Seven roads lead to Labastide-Murat, but the preferable approach from a southerly direction is by D.13 from Cabrerets to St. Martin-de-Vers and then by D.32. This bastide was called Labastide-Fortanière until renamed in honour of 'Le Roi Murat'—the cottage where he was born is now shown to tourists.

The most brilliant of Napoleon's marshals, Murat married the Emperor's sister Caroline, and became King of Naples. After the retreat from Moscow, during which he displayed extraordinary courage and endurance, he tried to save his throne by making a separate peace with the Allies, which Napoleon considered so venal that he refused his aid during the Hundred Days—although admitting too late that his presence might have turned the tide at Waterloo.

But while Napoleon was still on Elba, Murat was driven from Naples by the Austrians, escaped to France, and took refuge at Labastide-Murat in the château he had built there for his brother André. It was sound strategy to presume that no serious search would be made for him in so obvious a hiding place, but a trivial incident almost prevented it from succeeding—an incident vividly described to me by one of André's descendants.

On the morning that the search-party arrived, Murat's eight-year-old niece asked him to show her his sword, and she was playing with it when warning was received that a troop led by a captain was riding towards the château gates. As had been planned, Murat withdrew to an attic, and the captain was entertained by the rest of the family while his men made a perfunctory search of the house and garden.

All went well until the child's mother suddenly

noticed that the sword had been left on a table behind the chair in which the captain was sitting. Her agitation might not have communicated itself to anyone else if only she could have stopped staring at it. But stare at it she did! And when the others, who by now had seen the sword too, tried to distract her attention she made matters even worse by guiltily blushing. The captain cannot have been very observant, or else he did not realize the implications of the sword's presence, for he was about to lead his troop down the drive when, overwhelmed by relief, the silly woman fainted. This at last aroused his suspicions and he ordered his men to make a more thorough search. But from the attic window Murat had seen the cordon withdrawn and had seized the opportunity to reach the woods and safety.

We left Labastide-Murat by D.17 after lunching at the Poste et Boule d'Or—which has good food and a fine stone staircase in the older part of the hotel—as I had seen on the map that there is a *beau château* at Vaillac. The château is poised on a promontory above the village and, as we could not find a way to drive up, we left the car under a plane tree beside the church and took a steep path, which became increasingly overgrown until I almost agreed with Charles's view, that it would have been more sensible to ask the way rather than to set off purposefully in what might be the wrong direction. However, I panted on another few yards and suddenly came in sight of such a splendid guardian wall, such massive towers, that it would have taken a pair of hostile mastiffs to turn me back. A faded Propriété Privée was not discouraging, for experience had taught us that a request to look round is nearly always granted. But there was no one to ask, and we could not even peer through the lower windows for the glass was opaque with grime behind the rusty iron grilles.

The corner towers, each with a conical roof, and the

Ladies Walk, a wooden gallery jutting out at the fourth storey on the north and east face, date from an earlier period than the four tiers of Renaissance windows and the arches of the solar. The wide apron of turf on which Vaillac stands is walled on three sides, but to the south there is an open view for on this quarter the castle is defended by a precipice. Inside the western wall there is a long building which we first entered by a doorway partially blocked by earth and rubble that led to the kitchens, where the bread ovens could still bake for a large village, and the two hooded hearths are each wide enough to carry five cauldrons while roasting a sheep on a spit. Adjoining it are the stables, large enough for at least a hundred horses but empty now except for traces of cows.

We had to clamber up a ruined outside stair to reach the upper storey, and found ourselves in an enormous room where sunlight was streaming through eight shutterless windows on to a floor that was covered with a layer of chaff and old straw and fallen plaster.

"Mind where you step," said Charles, "The boards may be rotten; and look out for trap-doors or you may land in the stables."

"There won't be any trap-doors," I said emphatically, "for this wasn't used either as a hay-loft or as a granary. The men-at-arms and the male retainers slept here. There used to be partitions, lath and mud-plaster. I expect you can still see where they joined the main walls...and there would have been woollen curtains instead of interior doors...."

Charles was not listening, for he had gone into a watch tower and called me to look at the beams which supported the roof. "Like two wheels, one above the other, with the spokes extending beyond the rims to socket into the walls," he commented.

I displayed intelligent interest and then drew his attention to the privy in a tourelle, and pointed out that we now knew why the château itself had so many of these decorative little pepper-pots.

"A privy to each bedroom is an amenity seldom found in a modern Lotoise house," he said. "But as there is no moat the garden must have been very smelly especially in summer."

I felt illogically indignant. "It was not at all smelly! Each privy had a pit under it and fresh earth was thrown down them twice a day. When they were full they were dug out and the manure spread on the fields. It is only the ridiculous moderns who spoil the flavour of their vegetables and pollute their rivers—and even the sea—because they are too stupid to recognize the value of their own *merde*. And the pits were not even unsightly because they were concealed by bushes."

He laughed. "Well you needn't get so heated about it. Do you know all this, or are you guessing?"

I had to think for a moment before answering. "Half and half. I *don't* know what was done here, but I *do* know that this is what happened to the privies in the castle where I was born as Carola."

That Vaillac might well have been familiar with Italian usages in the sixteenth century became even more probable when we noticed that the carving on the façade of the belvedere is of that period and in the Italian manner. The ground floor is on the same level as the garden and a stair leads up to the flat roof from which the parapet has crumbled. I should have more greatly enjoyed the lovely view of the valley if I had been free from vertigo, and only when I had thankfully come down again did I notice a stair leading to an under-ground room in which I could see traces of frescoes which suggested it had been a chapel. I suddenly recalled why the name Vaillac had seemed familiar when I saw it on the map: Jacques de Colomb had told me about a woman who once lived there, so widely renowned for her charities that she was known as St. Fleur, although, so far as he knew, she was never beatified. I should like to have gone into her chapel, but as most of the treads had fallen it would have been a difficult climb and we might have been unable to get out again without a ladder.

There is another tower, rooted on a ledge of the crag, which I think must have been the eastern end of the walls where this defence is replaced by the precipice. The floorboards of the upper storeys, each a single room linked by a spiral stair, have gone; but the chimney-pieces and the jutting hearth-stones are still there, and so are the beams, which were casting heavy shadows on a stone floor, below ground level, that was lit by a narrow window cut through the face of the cliff.

Charles let himself down, by hanging by his hands from a beam, and then crouched to peer into a circular hole in the centre. "This is an oubliette," he announced, throwing down a piece of rubble to gauge the depth, "and this hole was the only way to get in or out of it, for there is no doorway...nor is there any trace of a window, and the only reason there is any light down there is because there has been a subsidence and the outer wall has cracked. It must be all of twenty feet deep; probably more, for there is a lot of debris."

He threw down a large piece of rubble, and jerked back as three enormous bats flew up from the hole, to circle so closely round my head that I was not sure whether I could feel their wings brushing my cheek or only the fan of their flying. Had I tried to dodge I should have fallen, for I was balanced precariously on a broken step. But fortunately I have felt friendly towards bats since Charles brought up an orphan batlet, with milk dropped into her mouth from a pipette. She was called Emily and lived for the next three months either in a drawer of his desk or his jacket pocket.

Charles was disappointed not to have had a better view of the bats, which were at least twice as large as any we had previously seen, but having failed to flush any more of them he remarked that it was annoying that we had no ladder, or even a rope, by which we could descend into the oubliette.

"If we stay here quietly for a bit the bats may come back," I said consolingly.

"I wasn't thinking about bats. I thought you would like to see if you could find any spooks down there. Only last week you were frustrated because you couldn't get into that other château to see if you could find anything in the oubliette."

I was rather pleased that he had thought I felt frustrated, for in fact I had been exceedingly relieved that we could not persuade the factor, in the owner's absence, to lend us the key. For in that oubliette seventeen Huguenot prisoners had died of starvation.

Jacques, during Sunday luncheon at Autoire, had mentioned them while extolling the château, which he said we might be able to rent very cheap because the owners seldom went there as it was haunted. "I know that nearly every château has dungeons where people have died," said Jacques, beaming through his spectacles, "but this oubliette may require Joan's attentions because the Huguenots did not starve until they had cannibalized each other."

He then discussed with vivid detail how unpleasant this diet must have been, especially with no cooking facilities; and I, trying to prove myself sufficiently robust for the topic not to impair my appetite, said that I was in no position to be fussy as I myself had been a cannibal.

"In some remote millennium I presume," said Jacques. And I, having stated that the experience occurred in March 1938, was forced to relate the episode.

I was the only guest, it being so early in the season, of a little hotel near Foix, in the foothills of the Pyrenees; and as the patron seemed lonely I suggested that we eat our dinner together. We started with *pâte de sanglier,* a specialité of the district made from wild boar. Towards the end of the meal I noticed that my companion was becoming increasingly distrait, but, thinking this was due only to the effort of comprehendng my French, I was startled when he burst into loud sobbing. And even more startled when he declared that he wept because he would soon be roasting in hell for the terrible sin of being a cannibal.

I presumed that he had been adrift after a shipwreck and had been driven by hunger to nibble a less enduring castaway, and so pointed out that unless he had also murdered his meal it was a matter of small importance. "He was probably delighted that you made good use of his body instead of wasting it on the fish," I added, patting his huge and heaving shoulder.

He paused between sobs to stare at me, bewildered. "I do not understand what you mean about the fish. I am weeping for the little *girl* I have eaten. And the sin is not mine alone, for you too are a cannibal!"

"Nonsense!" I said briskly, and then wondered if briskness was a tactless approach that would only make him angry.

But he was not angry, only sad; and tears were running down his jowls as he repeated stubbornly, "But, Madame, you *are* a cannibal! You cannot possibly deny it, for I myself have watched you eating my *pâte!*"

I found this alarming, for apparently I was not alone with a maniac, but with a maniac who tinned his victims. I was wondering if I had any chance of fleeing from the hotel before he added me to his larder, when he suddenly calmed down and said that if I would be kind enough to listen he would tell me the details of his pitiful story.

"*Sangliers* are sometimes dangerous," he began, after pouring each of us a large cognac, "but they seldom attack people unless they have been wounded or are savage with hunger after a hard winter. Yet only a month ago one of them killed a little girl—she was walking home from school through the woods, only three kilometres from my hotel. And it not only killed the little girl: it ate her...nearly all of her had it eaten when we found her body. And even her parents could recognize her only by her boots.

"The hunters followed the *sanglier's* tracks, but this was not easy for there had been a fresh snowfall. And although it must have stayed quite close to the village to digest its meal, they did not manage to shoot the murderous beast until they had searched and searched for three nights and two days.

"The carcase, as is our custom, belonged to the man who had shot it; but, although the meat of a young boar always fetches a good price, he said it should be buried. Everyone else agreed with him; but I, avaricious monster that I am, could not bear to see such a prize wasted. So I bought it from him, and dragged it back here—no one would help me, all alone, after nightfall, on a sled. And that very night I began to turn that accurséd flesh into a dozen large tins of my famous...my most *justly* famous, *pâte!*

"On my knees I implore you to believe that it was *after* I had heard you praise the contents of the first of these dreadful tins that I realized we had eaten not only the *sanglier* but the little girl who was inside him! It was you who noticed her first! Do you not remember? You said, when I pressed you to a second helping, that you would have to accept because my superb *pâté* had such a unique flavour!"

"What happened to the rest of the *pâté?*" inquired Jacques, with a relish that rebuked the diminished appetite of his other guests.

"My co-cannibal had convinced himself that the only way we could effectively shrive our sin was by going immediately to the cemetery—it was by then midnight—to bury the other tins in the child's grave. By stressing the likelihood of our being observed and probably mistaken for practitioners in the Black Art, I eventually persuaded him to accept my alternative plan, to do nothing until morning, when he would take the tins with him to Confession and leave the problem of their disposal to Monsieur le Curé."

"A very sensible solution." said Jacques approvingly.

"And while we are on the subject, I suggest that when you go in search of the cannibal Huguenots you had better make sure there is not a more recent phantom in the same château, a distant cousin of mine who died there shortly before the war. I did not know him well, for he spent most of his time in Paris, and when, on inheriting the title, he returned to the home of his ancestors, he became a recluse. He was not thought to be markedly eccentric until he dismissed all the family retainers, which of course made him most unpopular, and refused to see anyone except his old nurse who came every day from her cottage in the village. Then he barred the doors even to her, and she had to put his food in a basket—that always contained money to pay for the supplies of the previous day—which he let down on a rope from a fourth storey window of the Keep—the only part of the castle that is still inhabitable.

"This curious behaviour continued for about three years, until one day there was no basket. The old woman called to him increasingly loudly, and when he did not appear at the window she tried to get the villagers to help her break in; but all of them refused, saying that as Monsieur le Comte had been so un-friendly he deserved only to be ignored. After four days she went to the gendarmes, and they agreed to come with her to force the postern door. They found my poor kinsman lying on his great bed, and there was enough of his body left—the rest of it had been eated by rats—to show that he had died of starvation. But the rats had not only gnawed his bones, they had also gnawed holed in the mattress; and from it had flowed a hoard of gold coins hidden there before the Revolution...ten thousand Louis d'Or."

Chapter Twenty-four
THE DANCING YEARS

The interior of Vaillac is impressive because of the fine proportions of its great rooms, but less romantic than I had anticipated for it has been wantonly damaged by soldiers billeted there during the war, as we saw when we visited the château with Gillian and David and an obliging child from the village escorted me to the guardian of the keys. He is a most kindly man, but very difficult to find for his farm is about two kilometres up a turning opposite a chapel on the road to Labastide-Murat. The chapel is marked on the map, and although Michelin ignores the track—he usually acknowledges even 'paths for muleteers'—it is negotiable by car providing the driver does not object to reversing to the edge of a steep drop while rounding hairpin bends, or descending backwards should he meet an ox-cart. But despite these hazards—or even the effort of walking—it is worth going up there for the magnificent view of the castle, although even from this vantage point it cannot be photographed satisfactorily without a telescopic lens.

About the same distance from Vaillac there is an even wider view, of much easier access, at Cassagnoles— little more than a name on the map beside the sign which indicates a three hundred and sixty degree panorama. Cassagnoles is only two kilometres to the east of N.20, yet I doubt if one in a million of the motorists who use this great trunk road, which links Paris to the Spanish border, ever bother to turn off it at Pont de Rhodes, to refresh their spirit with the sense of freedom, the awareness of infinite space in which to grow, that comes from contemplating huge vistas flowing to the full circle of their horizon.

After our second visit to Vaillac, the four of us spent

an hour at Cassagnoles and then drove on towards Cahors, turning right on N.111 to dine at the Château de Mercuès. This château, perched on a cliff above what is, by comparison with the rest of the Lot, a mediocre reach of this lovely river, was built in the fourteenth century. It was besieged, unsuccessfully, by the English during the Hundred Years War, only to be pillaged and partially destroyed by fire in 1568 during the Wars of Religion. It was then restored, and became the seat of the Bishops of Cahors until 1906, when it passed into private ownership. It has retained much of its essential character although it is now a very good, sophisticated, hotel.

Mercuès is eleven kilometres from Cahors, where the Lot loops round the town and serves it as a moat, except at the north where there is a narrow isthmus which still has some of its original fortifications. The river is now spanned by only one of the medieval bridges which made it a 'jewel among cities'; but the Pont Valentré, with its three slender towers, its six great Gothic arches, its diamond-shaped buttresses, can still proudly maintain its right to be known as the most beautiful bridge in the world. It would have been tragedy enough if the other fourteenth-century bridge, and the even older Vieux Pont which had five towers instead of three, had been destroyed by besiegers; but it was by an enemy within the gates, an Idiocy of Town Councillors, that they were demolished, in 1868 and 1906, and replaced by pragmatical cast-iron.

The cathedral of St. Etienne, with its magnificent north door, and the little church of St. Urcisse, which has a most tender medieval Madonna and Child in a niche above the entrance, are in the older part of the town, where some of the streets are so narrow that even at noon they are in twilight. This is on the east of the wide Boulevard Gambetta, named, as are so many streets throughout France, after the famous democratic leader who became President of the *Chambre des*

The Madonna of St. Urcisse

Deputés and was Premier of France when he died, aged only forty-two. But he is honoured in Cahors not only for being born there, but for his audacity of escaping from the Siege of Paris in a balloon, an exploit of 8th October, 1870 which made headlines in the world's Press, and was shared by his secretary and Monsieur Nadar, the aeronaut, who accompanied him as he soared over the Prussian lines to land safely at Mont-didier. But to me even this romantic feat was of less importance than that he was Madame Rochet's grand-father. I discovered this fact when she was showing me the furniture that had belonged to him, then stored in the attic but now being used in the rooms of Les Tourelles, on the outskirts of Tour-de-Faure, which has become her hotel instead of only an annex to the Aux Bonnes Choses which she sold in 1960.

When Madame Rochet was satisfied that I would choose each melon, each peach, individually instead of merely asking for a kilo or a dozen; that I would prod and sniff twenty Brie if necessary before selecting the one that was at its moment of maturity, she entrusted me with commissions whenever we went to Cahors. The shortest route from the market place to the dairy which supplied her butter is by a narrow alley behind the police station, and I must have been along it many times without noticing that it contains a restaurant.

When Georges was our host there he seemed surprised that we had not already discovered the Restaurant de la Préfecture, and said reprovingly, "Surely you know that gendarmes always eat well?"

Our dinner confirmed his assertion, and we were warmly greeted by several policemen who had steered us through the complicated procedure of renewing our *permis de séjour,* which must be done after three months' residence unless a visa has been obtained before arriving in France. Getting the permit would have been much less involved had we remembered to do so before it was already a month overdue, and had not become known as professional authors who were also 'cousins' of Georges: this meant that for the honour of everyone concerned the letters of application must be impeccably written and adorned with the flowery phrases demanded when addressing a simple request in French to a *Chef du Bureau.*

As we drove homewards I was so sleepily replete that I almost protested when, at Savanac, Georges announced, "Turn left here. We will visit some cousins."

But Charles was wide awake, and the moment after he had carried out his instructions, Georges shouted "Stop!"

Charles would have stopped in any case, for the road had become a dance floor, walled on the right by a farm-house and on the left by a bandstand, made of planks laid across wine-barrels and draped with table-cloths under a red-and-white awning, and roofed by ropes garlanded with flowers and coloured electric light bulbs which made the scene gay as a Christmas tree.

The three bandsmen were playing vigorously, and, being dazzled by a spotlight which made their brilliantine glisten and the sweat on their foreheads glitter like sequins, failed to notice Georges until he walked purposefully forward to shake hands with the accordion player. The Clarinet and the Double Bass also broke off in mid-bar and waited expectantly for us to be introduced. The dancers showed no sign of annoyance at the interruption, but stared at us, whispering to each other, waiting patiently for the music to start again, no doubt knowing that Georges never permits himself to be hurried.

Having at last given the band permission to proceed, Georges conducted us through a gateway into a courtyard, where a pair of oxen stared drowsily at us from their stall, and then by an outside stair—on each step a pottery jar overflowing with orange, pink or magenta geraniums—to a vine-shaded terrace which served as a spectators' gallery.

After prolonged introductions and much hand-shaking with the village elders who were seated at a long trestle table, we were given glasses of ratafia which, as I dislike the taste, I drank as slowly as convention permitted, knowing that the moment my glass was empty it would be refilled. I was wondering how to discover which of them was our host, when Charles whispered that although this was a private house the owner sold wine and allowed the terrace to be used as a neutral meeting place by the people of the village, this being the obligation of the most prosperous member of a community which is too small to support even the most humble estaminet.

Charles tried to buy the next round of drinks, but was not allowed to pay for anything until about an hour later, when Georges accepted his suggestion that we might be allowed to show our appreciation by providing refreshment for the band. Until then the three musicians had kept up a continuous flow of fox-trots and tangos, for when one of them paused to take a gulp from the wine-bottle beside him the other two played even louder to fill the gap. The nearest we could get to 'champagne for the band' was three bottles of *vin mousseux*, but these were so well received by the musicians during a well-earned breather that when they started playing again it was with a much more stimulating rhythm.

Instead of feeling buffeted by the music I started to listen. This was real dance music, but what was it? Why was it so familiar? At first it reminded me of a Sardana, and then I realized I had not heard this lilt in Catalonia but in Scotland, when the piper was playing a reel. The woman who was sitting beside me said, "I see you enjoy the music of our *bourrée*. It is also a dance of the Auvergne, but we have our own variations which have been danced here for many hundreds of years." She sighed. "But soon no one will remember the *bourrée*, for the young people prefer fox-trots and refuse to learn such old-fashioned steps...and we, who know them, are too old to dance."

"Oh please dance it for us!" I exclaimed eagerly.

She shook her head. "It would be a happy thing to dance again, but I am too old. I am a grandmother."

"I am twice a grandmother, but I still dance when I feel inclined. I would so very much like to see you dance the *bourrée*."

Already her foot was tapping the rhythm under the table. I realized she was probably younger than I, although resigned to wearing the heavy strap-shoes, the thick lisle stockings, the funerary garments that constitute a peasant woman's 'Sunday Black.'

Her eyes were gay now and she was laughing. "Alphonse, pay attention!" she shouted to her husband. "The English friends of Georges Cabessut wish us to dance the *bourrée!*"

Alphonse had been talking to Charles, and did not seem too well pleased at the interruption. "I am too old to dance...and so are you, my old rabbit."

"She is not too old!" I exclaimed. "And neither are

you. You are both only old enough to have one grand-child, and I already have two."

This produced much friendly laughter, and I added, "Surely you are not afraid to show us the dance you have taken from our country? Or have you invented new steps for our Scottish music?"

"The *bourré* is *our* dance," they shouted.

"The music is the music of Scotland—but we play it with bagpipes."

"But we used to have bagpipes!" Now everyone joined in. Were there in Scotland two kinds of *bourré*, for four dancers and for eight? There were? Could there be—no, this would be too extraordinary even to imagine, a dance in which a man must place his steps between the blades of two swords?

"In Scotland I have seen a sword-dancer so agile, and so brave, that he turned the swords upwards and had the blades sharpened to a razor's edge, so that if he made one false step his foot would be gashed open."

"My grandfather has danced this sword-dance," cried Alphonse. "But I have never seen it."

I did not admit that I had seen it only through another man's eyes, those of Robbie Grant, who was the wisest gillie on Speyside.

Now talk flowed fast as the Lot flows when the high hills thaw at the end of winter. Gnarled hands thumped the table as though they sounded a dancing drum. Faces seemed to be wrinkled only by laughter; tanned not by hard endurance in the fields but through bask-ing under a gentle, genial sun.

"Yes, we will dance for you! But on one condition. You must dance for us first. Then if the young mock us we shall say, 'Is it only in England that dancing is permitted to grandmothers?'"

So dance we did, and the years fell away as they had done when, ten years ago, we found ourselves performing, also for illogical reasons, in a seedy Geneva night-club.

Then the *bourré* took up its lilt again and the four couples in their solemn black clothes wove the intricate patterns of the foursome and eightsome reels. The young people watched a little resentfully, but the children clapped their hands and shouted with joy. And when we went home at two o'clock in the morning, grandparents were still teaching grandchildren the magic of the *bourrée*.

We went to several fêtes, for nearly every week Thérèse and Colette, who were helping Madame Rochet during the season, reminded us that there would be dancing 'next Sunday' at some other riverside village; which was a hint that we should take them there in the car. They were both very good dancers; but Georges would not dance, even with them. "I cannot dance," he said, frowning as Thérèse or Colette whisked past him in the arms of another partner. "It is most annoying, but it makes me dizzy." Which is true, though surprising considering that Georges can climb an apparently perpendicular cliff with the expertise of a fly.

The setting for these village dances was sometimes almost unbelievably beautiful. At Calvignac after a day of heavy rain, the clouds suddenly cleared and left the village poised on its cliff above a world edged with black ribbon: storm over the horizon. Although there was no thunder the sky flickered with lightning, blue, yellow, and blue-white flames of summer; yet the air was so still that leaves from the young oak-trees which had been brought from the mountain-side to stand as a guard of honour at the war memorial, seemed to be made of white gold. I wandered off to watch from a distance. A bunch of coloured balloons like monstrous grapes from which was suspended a paper lantern, floated majestically up into the air until it seemed to join the stars. Then, as slowly, it descended and came to rest in the branches of a plum-tree. The sound of accordions seemed like water music, bubbling up from some source under the hill to flow down the steep little street before it tumbled gaily into the valley, now slowly filling up with river mist.

Georges came to look for me and we went farther up the hill to join Charles in a café. Not long after midnight Georges was tired, and said so. I eagerly agreed. "It is time we left...."

"We cannot leave without Thérèse and Colette. I promised their brothers I would look after them," he said gloomily. "They have not yet taken off their shoes. When they do so it will be a sign that they are at last beginning to tire."

At four o'clock they were still dancing, lively as the children who were still bouncing among the stalls like ping-pong balls, except for a few very young ones who had gone to sleep on some convenient lap. "My feet hurt," said Georges. "It is annoying that it is more tiring to the feet to stand than to walk long distances. Monsieur Beatty is still dancing. Englishmen must have very strong feet."

"I've been asleep on mine so long that I've forgotten what they feel like," I said. This rather puzzled him, for it is the kind of remark that sounds even more pointless when translated literally into French.

"Perhaps," said Georges wearily, "Monsieur Beatty would not mind if we waited for him in the car?"

"Of course he won't mind. I only wish I had thought of it sooner."

We had plodded half-way down the hill—for the car must have been about thirtieth in line on the roadside—when the band suddenly stopped playing and the others came running after us. "Calvignac does not give the band enough to drink," said Thérèsa apologetically. "They are already too tired to play any more. We looked after our band much better last week. At Tour-de-Faure they played until the sun came up."

"They look after the band well at Bouzies too," said Colette hopefully. "The dance will be there next Sunday...."

"I'll take you," said Charles. And, bless his heart, which is even stronger than his feet, he did.

Chapter Twenty-five
THE CHILDREN'S LOT

When I claimed to have suffered only from three fleas and a momentary brush with mosquitoes in the Lot, I had forgotten the horse-fly which flew into the car one evening as we were leaving Cahors, and bit me on the eyelid. We were within a mile of Larroque-des-Arcs where we were dining, and by the end of dinner my face was so hideously swollen that I thankfully retreated to a delightful bedroom—I think it is No. 11—at the end of the upper corridor of the Hostellerie Beau Rivage, where for three days I remained secluded, comforted by delicious meals, luxuriating in hot baths, and basking on the flat top of a truncated tower outside one of the three windows.

By our last evening I was fairly presentable in spite of a black-eye, but Charles, who had taken the car to Cahors to be serviced, was late getting back, so it was nine o'clock when we went down to the dining-room. Five other tables were still occupied by late arrivals who, judging by their clothes which were far smarter than we were used to seeing in the Lot, were breaking their journey on their way back to Paris.

We are just finishing our *écrevisses* when there enters a party of four adults and seven children. The eldest child is about eight years old and the youngest is a baby. While the soup is being served the baby wakes up and stares fixedly at the tureen. Mother, who has been preparing a bottle for him by mixing powdered milk with hot water from a thermos, exclaims, "Look! Look! At last Philibert has noticed what we are eating!"

Everyone at the table joins in the excitement.

"Philibert must have some soup in his bottle," clamour the brothers and sisters. "He wants it! He wants it!"

Mother, delighted, tips away half the formula and tops up the bottle with soup—good rich soup it is too, not the pallid broth which is all Philibert could have hoped for had he been born English. He has a good long suck at it, after Mother has enlarged the hole in the teat by prodding it with a hairpin; then he gazes round and loudly burps his approval.

Everyone is enchanted, including the occupants of the other tables, who beam or nod to show that they have noticed that yet another Frenchman has graduated from the dull business of mere eating to the appreciative enjoyment of appetite.

Half-way through the bottle Philibert is handed to Father, so that Mother can get at her soup before it grows cold. Father, knowing the drill, has emptied his plate quickly. By the time Philibert demands a second helping the soup-tureen has been taken away, so he is given a fragment of truffle omelette.

He is now drowsy, and is handed on from lap to lap round the table, a cosy variant of the dormouse at the Mad Hatter's Tea Party. He has nearly completed the circuit when he becomes sufficiently alert to enjoy bread-crumb soaked in the chicken's luscious sauce, which is affectionately fed to him by his eldest sister— and then goes serenely to sleep.

I was describing this incident to Madame Rochet— we were in the kitchen of the Aux Bonnes Choses—and happened to say that in a London restaurant no one would have appreciated Philibert, for in many of them children are considered somewhat out of place.

At first she thought I was joking, and then exclaimed indignantly, "When I had my little restaurant close to the *Chambre de Députés,* my clientèle was the most distinguished in Paris, but if I had not made the children welcome I should have lost all my customers in a week!" The thought of the appalling stupidity of

English restaurateurs caused her to glare into a stew-pan and to clash down the lid. "A restaurant without children, how can one imagine it! How can anyone hope to become a gourmet unless from his earliest years he is taught how to eat?"

That a civilized approach to the pleasures of the table can be acquired very early in life was exemplified on the following day, when nine children, unaccompanied by an adult came to the hotel for lunch.

The two eldest are girls of about ten, certainly no older. The others are considerably younger; the smallest boy is about three and has to be lifted on to his chair which has had its seat elevated by a hassock. We know some of the children by sight, for their parents have a house in the village to which they come in the summer holidays; the others are their guests who arrived yesterday.

Enter Madame Rochet. She embraces the taller girl, Ginette, who introduces her to those of the party she has not yet met, and Ginette then announces, "All our parents have gone out for the day so my mother thought it would be nice for us to have our luncheon with you."

Madame Rochet declares that she is enchanted at the pleasure of their company, and reads aloud the menu. Is it to their liking or would they prefer her to prepare something different? There is Hors d'Oeuvres; Tripes; Bœuf en Daube; Stuffed Tomatoes. Will that be enough? A salad perhaps before the fruit? The children nod as each item is mentioned. They agree that they will have everything; the salad too. And could there be an ice as well as the fruit? Certainly there can be an ice. Coffee or Vanilla?

The children seat themselves and tuck their napkins expectantly under their chins, that of the smallest being tied round his neck by an attentive and only slightly older brother. With unhurried courtesy they hand dishes of hors d'oeuvres to each other, placing olive stones and radish stalks in a neat row on the edge of their plates. With complete decorum they remain absorbed by the joys of eating for the next hour and a half.

Only then does the smallest child, whom I had been watching with some anxiety fearing he would either have to be sick or burst, give a deep sigh of repletion and doze off, after resting his head carefully on the table so as not to upset a wine-glass—they all drank wine mixed with their mineral water, the proportion graduated according to their age. A few moments later he awoke, refreshed by his nap and still enchantingly amiable. They all filed into the kitchen to thank Madame Rochet and compliment her on the excellence of the menu; queued beside the basin in the hall to wash their unsticky hands and faces, and then, when we expected to see them process sedately down the street, suddenly burst into an exuberance of energy, running and shouting and clambering over the rocks and being as boisterous as any English children could have been.

The first time I saw a newly born baby brought into a Lotoise estaminet I was surprised when young men, tough men, men so old that their joints creaked as they rose from the table, crowded round it, jostling each other for a closer view. But Frenchmen genuinely admire babies, and when one is offered for inspection it is essential to make some appropriately flattering remark; to which everyone will listen and which by nightfall will have been repeated throughout the village.

Charles solved this problem by using the phrases employed by Irishmen when trying to sell a rather doubtful horse. "What a bold eye he has!" gained him considerable kudos, for it was taken to mean that in due course it would sire many more bold babies. "Look at the great shoulders on him!" foxed the audience for a minute, as well it might for all that was visible was its little muffin-like face. Then the father broke into shouts of delighted laughter and declared Charles had forecast the fulfilment of his secret ambition, that his son would wear the Yellow Jersey, the gage of victory in the Tour de France bicycle race. On a later occasion he tried, "She will be the best little filly that ever looked through a bridle!" But this fell rather flat, understandably as I have not yet seen anyone on horseback in the Lot.

Lotoise children are allowed to eat, or not to eat, as they feel inclined, but, even more important, they are not sent to bed when they have no desire to sleep. At a village fête it is normal to see children bubbling over with vitality at three o'clock in the morning, and I have walked in St. Céré at midnight, where except in the holiday season everything closes at 10 p.m., and seen children playing hide-and-seek among the sheeted horses of a merry-go-round long after their parents have gone to bed. The reason they can do this without getting tired is that they take a nap whenever they need one. Anywhere will do: a haycock, or the maize stalks in the back of an ox-cart, or a coat under a bench in an estaminet, and for the babies there are always plenty of laps.

When I mentioned to a friend of Hugette's that English children had a fixed bedtime she stared at me in astonishment. "But how can that be so? My eldest son is only three, but if I *told* him when he ought to go to bed it would be more unkind than if I made him wear nappies now that he can announce when he desires to make peepee!"

It is not mere pride in paternity which makes these men so adept at handling babies, but because they have been brought up to regard the opposite sex as a complement instead of as an inferior or a rival. I have often seen a boy giving a bottle to a younger member of the family or changing its nappy, and even the toughest of them has no fear of being thought a cissy if he offers a little girl a bunch of flowers; although Charles, when he first saw this preliminary wooing, said rather cynically that the boy must have come from a family of restaurateurs and so known that however high the chef's bonnet it is almost invariably his woman who actually cooks.

The girls accept their posies with becoming modesty, but know themselves worthy of this masculine tribute for from a very early age they have taken trouble to please. Most graphically was this demonstrated by two little girls whom we met while walking beside the stream which feeds the waterfall above Autoire.

They were talking earnestly together, the younger pleading for a favour which the elder withheld. As the larger was certainly no more than nine years old, and the smaller about three, and it must have been a long trudge for them up the steep hill from the village, I thought the little one was imploring her sister to carry her home, a service which Charles would willingly perform.

Thinking that it might be easier for them to accept our assistance if they thought that adults, moreover foreign adults who sometimes deliberately walk when they might ride, could also admit to being exhausted, I announced as we came within earshot, and not without honesty, that I found myself to be enormously fatigued.

They heard me and looked up, politely smiling. We offered sweets, which they accepted. We engaged them in conversation: on the prevalence of wild flowers, the pleasant sound of the waterfall, our friendship with Monsieur le Marquis and his so charming mother and wife: this so that they should not take us for kidnappers when I suggested that we should return together to the village.

Charles was about to add that he would be honoured if they would take turns in riding on his shoulders when the elder said apologetically, "I regret, Madame, that we are not yet ready to return home. We shall be fully occupied for at least another hour." She paused to look sternly at her sister. "We shall have to stay here for at least two hours if she wriggles."

At this the little one chirruped, "I will keep still! I promise!" And showing no signs of fatigue pranced round us chanting, "Antoinette is going to make my hair look pretty! Antoinette is going to give me lots and lots of beautiful curls."

Antoinette rebuked her for this unseemly display of exuberance, and then took from the pocket of her blue pinafore a comb and a packet of hairpins which she set out carefully on a ledge of rock. She dipped the comb in the stream and ran it through the child's hair to damp it, saying, "Now lie down and put your head in my lap, and keep *still*...or I shall have to bite you."

Then, perhaps conscious that threats should never be necessary to maintain discipline, she added gently, "You must keep still as a little dead bird so that I can make you look pretty."

She began curling the silky, maize-coloured hair expertly round her finger, setting each curl in place with a pair of interlaced hairpins. She was so absorbed in her task that we might suddenly have become invisible; but as we got up to leave she smiled up at me and said, "My little sister had been so naughty that our mother said she must go with straight hair to the fête tomorrow. But why should the boy who loves her be disappointed that she has no curls?"

Chapter Twenty-six
STATION SOUFFLÉ

The first seventy-five kilometres of the Lot, upstream from Cahors, has a road on each side, and it is difficult to decide whether to choose the high or the low, the left or the right bank, when beginning the journey to its source in the Massif Centrale for they are equally lovely and join at Pont-de-la-Madeleine.

The next stretch is less attractive because of its proximity to the zinc mines of Decazeville, and is best avoided by following N.122 through Figeac to Maurs-la-Jolie and N.663 to Port d'Agres, whence another 36 kilometres of serene riverside road leads gently to Entraygues.

Here the Truyère flows into the Lot and the pleasant little town has two fine bridges; but its chief claim to fame was its site at the lower end of the gorge, when the Lot, between Entraygues and Estaing, thrust its way through a cleft in the mountains with a splendid turbulence of cascades. But it does so no longer, and when I went back there with Denys, I could have wept to see the wild river in the process of being tamed to the drab service of a hydroelectric power station.

The reason why the girls of Estaing seldom have short hair is that this would disqualify them from figuring as angels, let alone being chosen to represent the Madonna, at the fête on the first Sunday of July, when the highlight is the procession to the church, some dressed as the Heavenly Host and others as pilgrims to the shrine of St. Jacques de Compostelle, or as members of the family of d'Estaing.

The d'Estaings are included, not because of a lingering feudalism but because the Bienheureux François d'Estaing, whose statue stares from the bridge at the castle where he was born, was a Renaissance saint who

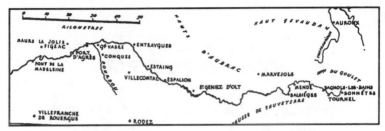

The River Lot from its origin to Figeac

built the great tower of Rodez Cathedral out of his revenues as its bishop.

Rodez is only about 40 kilometres from Estaing, either by following the Lot to Espalion and then taking N.120 and N.88; or by the route I prefer, D.22 to Villecomtal and then south on N.604. The cathedral was begun on 25th May, 1277, on the site of an older church, and continued to grow for the next three centuries. It is magnificent but not magical, although it might have been so had music been pouring from its unique organ, whose case of incredibly buoyant carving soars like a cantata in silver and wood.

When Charles and I went to Rodez it was not primarily to see the cathedral, but because after three days of exploring by-roads in the Montagnes d'Aubrac, and finally attempting one which dwindled into a logging track so narrow and precipitous that it took four hours to negotiate, we wanted the unaccustomed luxury of a room with a bath.

This was easy enough to find, for it was late in the season; but the water was tepid, and when we came downstairs, clean but uncomforted, we were told that dinner would be served punctually at seven-thirty— which was in five minutes. A glance into the empty dining-room where, pallid as monstrous mushrooms, the cloths of unlaid tables gleamed in the gloom, gave us the incentive to escape. Where should we eat? We would walk until we found somewhere. So we walked and walked, seeing first a restaurant that was closed for the day, and then another which was so full of lucky people sitting on comfortable chairs and eating and drinking, that there was no vacant place for us to do these desirable things, unless we waited for at least an hour. Something must be done to amend our situation immediately, for Charles also was tired and thirsty and so potentially fretful. I tried to visualize the relevant page of the *Guide Michelin* which I had left in the hotel. Had there been a restaurant marked with a star in Rodez? The shadowy image became a little clearer. Yes, there was such a restaurant—somewhere near the station. Perhaps it was called the Hotel de la Gare.

Charles was not enthusiastic, for to reach the station, which is on the northern fringe of the town, we should have to plod back nearly a mile to fetch the car. He was even less enthusiastic when I tried to take a short cut which led us far into uninhabited country before the road at last became wide enough for the car to turn round. It was after nine when we reached the station. Charles looked searchingly in every direction and then exploded. "No hotel! No restaurant! Not even a bar! Search this bloody goods-yard if you must, but don't expect me to come with you."

"The place may have been called the Buffet de la Gare," I said despairingly: but he didn't answer.

Leaving him glaring at nothing through the windscreen, I hurried away, praying that at least I might find a bottle to placate him. We could drink out of tooth-glasses and have a picnic in our room...I was almost sure there was an unopened tin of *pâté* and half a loaf and the remains of a Camembert lurking among the luggage in the back of the car.

The station was dark except for a light in the booking office.

Then I noticed a reddish glow on the far side of the yard—light shining through red curtains. It might be a buffet, and still open. We might at least get a drink even if it were too late for any food. My heart quickened as I drew closer. Geraniums in window boxes: improbably, I pushed open the door and stood incredulous for a moment before shouting for Charles. He too blinked as though he could not trust his eyesight when he stood with me on the threshold. Champagne-coolers sparkled between gilt baskets of fruit on a huge sideboard. The enormous looking-glass over the black marble chimney-piece reflected a scene that was as cosily Edwardian as a bustle or a straw boater.

Thankfully we sank into chairs at the nearest table. There were perhaps twelve tables, with cloths as smooth as the apron of an old-fashioned Nanny. At five of them people were eating—and not with the drab purposefulness of travellers who cram food into themselves as though the stomach were no more than a carrier-bag; but savouring each mouthful with dedicated relish as Shakespeare might have savoured the sweet syllables of a sonnet.

Madame Fraux, the priestess of this sanctuary, advanced upon us. She welcomed us as old friends—which we became in two minutes. What would we like to eat? We said it was for her to choose—for this seemed more courteous than to ask directly what was available in the kitchen. She gave us a menu, a menu on which were the names of at least forty noble dishes, and left us to brood over it while our bodies caught up with the rise in our spirits by being given large brandies and sodas.

"She says," said Charles in an awed voice, "that we can have anything on the menu. It's so impossible that I'm inclined to believe it."

He started with a dozen snails and I with a *truite meunière*, and both were gastronomic perfection. Then we had *cervelles au beurre noire*, two sets of brains each, the convolutions unbroken, the black butter exact, the capers neither too sparse nor over dominant.

Then Charles had veal in an admirable sauce, while I had the best *rognons à la brochette* I have ever tasted, each morsel of kidney scented with herbs before being interleaved on the skewer with bacon. We were full by now but still gloriously greedy. We had seen six superb soufflés carried to other tables, each rising from its silver dish with a gay insouciance that the ones I attempt never achieve. Could any chef make seven such soufflés in a row? This one could—and did. It was large enough for at least six people, but we managed nearly all of it after I had unabashedly undone the waistband of my skirt.

We stayed there, too happy and replete to move, until after midnight. We thought the bill when it came would be enormous, but what did we care? "Whatever the cost we could not have had a better meal anywhere in France," said Charles, "which is to say, in the world."

"And the service was worthy of the food," I agreed ecstatically.

We should have been almost overburdened with bliss had we then known that the total bill, including the brandies and soda already mentioned, two carafes of superior wine, one white and one red, three lots of coffee and a pair of Armagnacs, would be less than three pounds.

Benignly we watched diners come and go, none of them in a hurry, each placidly appreciative that eating can be an art. When the other guests did not require her attention Madame Fraux sat with us at our table. She showed me the kitchen, a room not much wider than a passage, in which her husband and son-in-law produced faultless dishes that could not have been bettered with ten times their equipment and a *brigade de cuisine* of twenty chefs. I told her with complete sincerity that I had never eaten better—not even before the war at Laperouse.

We were talking of soufflés when I remembered that they are supposed to go flat if anyone so much as bangs an oven door. "It must be very annoying," I said, "if a train stops at the station when your husband is making a soufflé."

She laughed. "Many trains stop here, but they know about my Buffet. I won the gold medal for the best in France."

"But I haven't heard a train since we came in, and that is more than three hours ago," said Charles.

She drew back the curtain from one of the windows which flanked the sideboard and stood, smiling at our astonishment, as we peered out. A train was drawn up at the platform within six yards of us, a proud passenger train, of the kind whose arrival and departure demand pandemonium: yet all was silence. It was like seeing a ghost train. Porters were setting down suitcases as though they were paper bags of plovers' eggs. Crates were moved stealthily, as though by burglars in bedroom slippers. Carriage doors were closed without a sound, as though behind them a baby slept, which would have to be rocked to sleep again by anyone clumsy enought to waken it.

I felt as though I was either dreaming or watching a film whose sound-track was out of action. The guard raised his trumpet, about to give an ear-splitting toot to signal the trains's departure. Then he remembered that he was outside the Buffet de la Gare at Rodez. His arm fell to his side. If the light had been brighter I might have seen him blush. It was not Madame Fraux who had reminded him of his obligations to gastronomy but his own train. The engine, which had been holding its breath for ten minutes, let out a sibilant whisper of steam. "Hush!" it insisted. "HUSH! HUSH! Hush...hush, hush, hush." And the long line of obedient carriages, like good children on tiptoe, crept out of the station on velvet wheels.

Chapter Twenty-seven
THE SAINT AND THE SINNERS

The great abbey of Conques and its magnificent medieval treasure is thirty-six kilometres north-north-west of Rodez by N.601, a road which then follows the Dourdou for another six kilometres through the gorge until it joins the Lot, twenty-three kilometres downstream of Entraygues.

The first character in the long history of Conques is Dadon the Hermit, who must have chosen this harsh, arid valley to ensure solitude for his mystical meditations which, not long after his death, caused Louis le Débonnaire to issue, in 819, a royal charter for the foundation of a monastery on the site of his hermitage. Thirty years later, Pépin II, King of Aquitaine, donated further domains which included Figeac and rich valley lands of the river Célé. These lands were farmed by monks from Conques, who established thereon a second community which within forty years had become so prosperous that the parent monastery would have been abandoned except for the ingenuity of a monk called Ariviscus.

Inspired either by a sincere belief that his present dour surroundings were the more suitable soil for the cultivation of the spirit, or a determination not to be outdone by the material efficiency of rival brethren, Ariviscus recognized that Conques's survival depended on its ability to attract pilgrims. It already had one advantage, an inaccessibility which would cause the pilgrim to feel that he had acquired merit merely by the effort of getting there, and so already be sufficiently freed from his sense of unworthiness to be able to accept a blessing. But it lacked the essential factor, being neither the site of a renowned miracle nor in the possession of a miraculous relict. For instance, a relict

205

such as was possessed by the monks of Agen . . . .

So Ariviscus went to the monastery of Agen, posing as a secular pilgrim who wished to work there as a lay brother. He was accepted, and after several years as a postulant took vows and was allowed to take his turn in guarding the relicts of Sainte Foy, a girl who at the age of twelve had been martyred at Agen on 6th October, 303.

Sainte Foy must have recognized that Ariviscus had true faith in her powers, for instead of being offended when he forced open her tomb and fled from the monastery carrying in a sack the charred remains of the body she used to inhabit, she afforded him magical protection, hiding him with mist and employing thunder and cloudbursts to baffle his pursuers.

She arrived at Conques with Ariviscus on 4th January, 866, and found her new environment so congenial that pilgrims in ever increasing numbers came to seek her aid and richly rewarded the guardians of her beneficence. When, in 980, she restored sight to a pilgrim called Guibert, who had been blinded by having his eyes torn out, her miracles became renowned throughout Christendom, bringing such lavish tribute that during the following century the abbey grew to the full splendour of its stature.

The tide of pilgrims flowed steadily to Conques until the thirteenth century and then began to ebb; for it was becoming difficult even for the most devout to maintain the faith required to manifest miracles when sainthood was so unjustly associated with the policy of a Church which throughout the Midi was performing abominations not only against a rival sect but against the fundamental Christian ethic.

The victims were the Cathari, literally the pure, who held it to be their duty to protest against corruption, either in the Church or in the social order, and believed that only the perfected in spirit were ready to enter Paradise while the vast majority of mankind, including the members of their own faith, still required physical reincarnation. Even more heretical was their refusal to join crusades, on the grounds that killing fellow-humans, even if they happened to be infidels, was incompatible with the specific instructions that it is the basic duty of man to learn how to love his neighbour.

The Pope, Innocent III, was keenly aware that the teaching of Jesus must not be allowed to interfere with the authority of the Church—especially the teaching of reincarnation which had only been declared a heresy in the fifth century on the grounds that it undermined the power of the priests over the people; so, as the Sixth Crusade was about to set off for the Holy Land for another round with the Saracens, he re-routed it to the Comté of Toulouse with instructions to exterminate heretics at home instead of abroad. No doubt most of the crusaders were relieved that the religious beliefs of their new opponents did not allow them to fight back or even to defend themselves; and if the more chivalrous knights had qualms, they could console themselves with the thought that only fifty years earlier the Blessed Saint Bernard had decreed, "The Knight of Christ kills with a clear conscience and dies in the greater tranquillity. In dying he finds his own salvation, and in killing he is doing the work of Christ."

The King of France, Philip Augustus, cannot have been pleased by the prospect of foreign soldiery massacring large numbers of his people whose tenets made them model citizens and tax-payers, but there were two reasons why he dared not protest. The majority of the French Cathari—there were seventy-two sects of them in Europe—were in the Comté of Toulouse which was ruled by the most powerful and the most rebellious of the remaining feudal overlords, who, had he not been otherwise engaged, might have joined forces with King John and helped England and Aquitaine to retain their French possessions.

Even more important than this counsel of expediency was Philip's personal experience of the power of Innocent III, who had excommunicated him for repudiating his second wife, Ingeborg of Denmark, although he had never seen her until the marriage which he was unable to consummate because she aroused in him so violent an antipathy that he could not bear her even to be in the same room. When excommunication failed to bring him to heel, the papal interdict was extended to the entire population, which meant that throughout France there were no religious ceremonies whatsoever, nor Extreme Unction, nor Burial Service; a state of affairs which continued for eight months, until on 8th September, 1200, for the sake of his people and his throne, the King had to overcome his squeamishness.

Philip was ashamed of being squeamish, for when he was in Syria on the Fifth Crusade it had caused him to flee in terror from the epidemic caused by the rotting corpses of six thousand decapitated prisoners, so leaving Richard Coeur-de-Lion, the son of his father's first wife, seriously in the lurch. So he was thankful to leave the fate of the Cathari to Simon de Montfort, a minor noble who was put in charge of field operations by Raymond VII, Count of Toulouse; but as a demonstration of his royal approval he sent his son, who later became Louis VIII, to take part in the later stages of this ruthless suppression of pacifism.

On 21st July, 1209, Simon de Montfort opened the campaign by directing the massacre of seven thousand men, women and children at Béziers. During the next fifteen years at least a hundred thousand more Cathari were slaughtered: the less unfortunate dying by rope, fire or sword; the rest set free to die slowly, the males having been emasculated to ensure that they should not breed more heretics,which seems a needless precaution considering that their eyes had been put out, their ear-drums pierced by red-hot wires, their teeth wrenched from their jaws and their hands lopped off at the wrists.

Yet the fanatical sadism of Simon de Montfort was not satiated even by such torrents of blood; for in 1219, when the garrison of Marmande—a little town of five thousand inhabitants near the confluence of the Lot and the Garonne—had surrendered and he was holding a council of war with the Dauphin about their disposal, it only required a bishop to stand up and demand that all should be killed as heretics for him immediately to agree.... "At once the hue and cry was raised. Soldiers poured into the town with drawn swords and the butchery began. Heads, dismembered bodies, limbs, brains, entrails, piled up in the streets as though they had rained from the sky. Everywhere the ground was red and saturated with blood. Except for the very few who succeeded in remaining hidden, neither man nor woman, either young nor old, survived: and the dreadful shambles was then destroyed by fire."

The Cathari had been most numerous in the neighbourhood of Albi—which caused them also to be known as the Albigenses—and when their persecution abated, through lack of further victims, only to be succeeded by the tortures of the Inquisition, the townspeople at last revolted and hunted their bishop into his cathedral from which he excommunicated them *en masse*. So when Bernard de Castanet became Holy Inquisitor for the diocese he built a new cathedral at Albi which, with its adjoining palace could serve as a fortress to protect him from their wrath. When they at last appealed to the King for protection, a cohort of bishops was sent from Paris to conduct an ecclesiastical inquiry, and removed Bernard—by promoting him to the See of le Puy where he died a cardinal.

Although the architectural glories of the Cathedral and Bishop's Palace of Albi are such that it now seems more apposite to liken the colour of the soaring brick walls to faded roses rather than faded blood, it must have been most aggravating for the Chapter of Conques to have such adverse publicity emanating from a bish-

209

opric only sixty miles away as the carrion-crow flew. The monks, like the pilgrims, dwindled in number, and by 1424 only twenty-eight remained and so the great abbey was deemed redundant and deconsecrated.

The monastic buildings must have been used for some secular purpose, for the treasure remained at Conques, and was successfully hidden from the Protestants who, in 1568, tried to get their hands on it, and failing, set fire to the nave of the abbey. The treasure was again hidden during the Revolution, when the mayor received warning that the Republican Officials, who had just finished looting the Cathedral of Rodez, were on their way to his village to continue their work of melting down church treasure into coin, as was being done throughout France.

The mayor assembled his people and divided the treasure among them, making each family responsible for an individual piece. When the Republicans arrived, saying that Conques could now have the honour of participating in the glorious Revolution, he replied, feigning regret, that they had celebrated their Revolution the previous week by zealously stripping the abbey of every object of value. So the Republicans went away without protest, no doubt recognizing that wresting loot from the tough local peasantry, who for centuries had been adept at hiding their small possessions from tax-gatherers and abbey-bailiffs, would be a far more dangerous undertaking than commandeering it from dispirited churchmen. When the Terror was over each family brought back to the mayor the piece which had been entrusted to them, which is why Conques still has one of the few medieval treasures that exist anywhere in the world.

Chapter Twenty-eight
A FEAST OF FISHES

Except for a beneficent thunderstorm, which broke with such torrential force as we reached Grand-Vabre that it was impossible to see through the windscreen, Denys and I would have gone on to Conques for the night instead of stopping at the Gorges du Dourdou.

As though the storm had not already been providential enough in providing us with a warm welcome, and a dinner which included a *poulet aux olives* so excellent that I was taught how to make it the following morning, it had a far greater marvel in store. We were drinking our coffee and darkness had fallen behind the steel rods of rain, when suddenly the dining-room was flooded with a scarlet glow. Our hostess came running from the kitchen thinking the house was on fire, and the only other female guest flung her arms round a stranger at the next table and implored him to comfort her during the last hour of the world.

Leaving him to this apparently congenial task we went outside, to find the sky bright as noonday but a brilliant glowing rose instead of blue. Yet it shed no light on the crags, sharply silhouetted as though carved from black basalt. The rain had ceased, and only the metallic note of drops still falling from the stone roof plucked the profound silence. Then a double rainbow spanned the gorge, its radiance undimmed until, abruptly as though a celestial stage-hand had turned the master switch, the scene vanished.

After this glory, even the treasure of Conques seemed somewhat of an anti-climax, although the gold, jewel-encrusted statue of Sainte Foy, made in 985, as a new reliquary for her bones, which are now behind the abbey's High Altar, has a brooding frustrated power which chills the spine, even though the idol stares from its bedizened golden throne through a flood-lit glass case which dominates the museum in the cloisters. Usually one can enjoy the treasure in peace, as I had done on my previous visit, but we were unlucky enough to be seized upon by one of the lay brothers who act as guides, a German, who refused to reply toDenys in that language and instead gabbled incomprehensible English further obscured by a glutinous Irish brogue. I still do not know whether the phrase which punctuated his diatribe was the Holy Fate, or Fête, or Faith, but it was still pounding against our ear-drums as we escaped into the sunlight.

Having already discovered that the Lot gorges were being devasted by bulldozers, and not wishing to revisit Estaing or Espalion, we left Conques by D.42 and for the next seventy-two kilometres of our homeward journey continued parallel to the river by D.20 and N.88, rejoining it at St. Geniez-d'Olt. Olt is the Celtic form of Lot, which the people of St. Geniez retain as a reminder that they stem from the pre-Roman stock; and its chief claim to fame is the Fête des Fraises, which takes place in June at the height of the strawberry season.

N.88 is soon following the river below the desolate Causse de Sauveterre which, like the countryside on the north bank, was de-forested two hundred years ago to rid it of wolves. Wolves had preyed on the sparse population for centuries, before, in 1765 one of them devoured so many scores of women and children that the people decided it must be a werewolf and appealed to the King for protection.

The finest marksman in France at last managed to shoot the Beast of Gévaudan with a silver bullet, and by royal command the body was taken to Versailles, where Louis XV declared himself astonished that it looked no different to that of any ordinary wolf. This was naïve of him, for he should have known that when a warlock dominates his familiar by remote control he produces no physical change in the animal, although by acting on its psyche he can intensify its natural instincts or even radically alter its behaviour—a misuse and extension of the same faculty possessed by people who have an 'uncanny knack with animals', exemplified in the jealously guarded Irish secret of the Horseman's Word. If the warlock is activating the link with his familiar when the animal is killed an echo-wound not infrequently appears in the human partner of this unsavoury alliance. Another hazard for the warlock is that he is likely to get trapped in his own black magic and so cannot avoid assuming the guise of his familiar when he becomes a ghost.

While I was in County Wexford I heard, from several sincere and sober sources, of whom two were hard-riding Catholics, of a silver bullet being used to prevent their recently deceased M.F.H. from continuing to hunt his hounds on moonlit nights. This had become a serious problem, for the sound of his horn disturbed the sleep of his erstwhile companions, and far worse, in the morning their horses were found lathered in sweat, apparently galloped to a standstill and too exhausted to leave the stables.

Fortunately the local Curé was himself a keen horseman, and having failed to abate the nuisance by more orthodox means, he melted down six Georgian teaspoons and moulded them into a silver bullet for a .22 rifle. Thus armed, on the next full moon he waylaid the phantom hunt, and although he could only hear the horn and the belling of the pack his aim must have been accurate, for Master and hounds departed to happier hunting fields.

It seems probable that at least one modern French sculptor also believes in werewolves, so horrific is the statue of the Beast of Gévaudan at Marvejols, a bastide with three fortified gates in the mountains nine kilometres north of the river. Still farther upstream, at Balsièges, we had turned south the previous year to

213

explore the country of the Tarn gorges. This is dramatic but malevolent, especially the savage Causse Noir in the vicinity of Montpellier-le-Vieux, where the rock formations resemble Dracula castles in which vampires would undoubtedly lurk in the bed curtains and weremastiffs prowl the corridors further to discourage guests.

We went to the cathedral at Mende, but having neither heard nor seen the bells—except a cracked one on the floor at the end of the nave—I was surprised to read later that they are included in the 'Four Marvels of the Midi', the other three being the belltower of Rodez, the Cathedral of Albi, and the Abbey of Conques.

I am uncertain whether it is before or after leaving N.88, to follow the left bank of the Lot to Bagnols-les-Bains, that there is laburnum instead of the ubiquitous acacia among the pine woods: but I shall always remember the clarion of their strident yellow pennants among the sombre trunks.

Beyond Bagnols-les-Bains, a little spa whose medicinal springs were also considered restorative by the Romans, the road goes through a tunnel under the great castle of Tournel, a ruin splendidly evocative of bold barons. Then a stony track turns off the main road to end at the hamlet of Bonnetés in the Montagne du Goulet, close to the source, at four thousand feet, of the Lot.

We were tired when we got there, but the strong sunlight, the clean wind surging over the Cevennes, the huge horizons, poured energy into us; and by the time we had returned to N.88 and were following it beside the Chapeauroux, Denys decided he wanted to ensure trout for dinner before arriving at the Hotel du Commerce, where we had stopped for lunch at Auroux on our way to the Tarn gorges, and been so impressed by the virtues of Madame Bernard's cooking that we lingered for a blissful week.

I had watched Denys cast many flies on the Chapeauroux, which pours through wooded defiles,

214

turbulent as a Highland river, on its steep descent to join the Allier, and there were occasions when even the pleasure of collecting flowers and fungi, or the sound and sight of waterfalls, failed to distract my attention from the fact that I was ankle-deep in a chilly march.

But on this evening I had the grace of unalloyed affection. "Please let him have trout for his supper," I said urgently to the Invisible. "Two large ones or four small, whichever You find the more convenient."

The response was immediate and unequivocal: "He shall have fish."

So I was dismayed and bewildered when, after about an hour, Denys put up his rod, saying he had not even seen a rise, much less had a nibble. Even a tumultuous welcome from Madame Bernard failed to dispel my profound disquiet. Undoubtedly we would have a splendid dinner, including her succulence of pigeons: but she too had had to apologize for the absence of trout.

Diminished, I unpacked all we should need until tomorrow, when two hundred and eleven kilometres through le Puy and Montfaucon would bring us to Lyon in plenty of time to catch the Car-Sleeper Express. The bedroom was unaltered—even the string I had put up to hold Denys's ties was still tacked to the wardrobe door—but it was no longer scented by the narcissus we used to gather in armfuls from the drifts which in the distance looked as though snow still lingered on the mountain slopes.

We were fortifying ourselves with cognac and Perrier before dinner, and I was trying to assure myself that somehow I should contrive not to falter even though a hunch had proved ephemeral as material possessions, when Madame Bernard came running to show us four fat trout, their scales bright as raindrops in their cradle of grass.

"A gipsy brought them for you," she said. "A child, and he vanished before I could give him any money."

JOAN GRANT'S WRITINGS

Additional copies of *A Lot To Remember* may be purchased at your favorite bookstore or directly from the publisher, Ariel Press. The book sells for $10.95 plus $2 for shipping. On orders of 5 or more copies, the price is $9 plus $5 for shipping.

Also available from Ariel Press is the entire series of Far Memory novels by Joan Grant, as well as her autobiography, *Far Memory* (originally published as *Time Out of Mind*). These eight books may be bought as a set for $75, postpaid. Or they can be purchased individually. The titles and prices of the set are:

Winged Pharaoh — $9.95.

Life as Carola — $9.95.

Return to Elysium — $9.95.

Eyes of Horus — $11.95.

The Lord of the Horizon — $9.95.

Scarlet Feather — $10.95.

So Moses Was Born — $9.95.

Far Memory — $9.95.

Be sure to add $2 postage per book for each title ordered individually. These prices are subject to change.

To order, send a check or money order to Ariel Press, P.O. Box 1387, Alpharetta, GA 30239. For fastest service, call us toll free at 1-800-336-7769 and charge your order to MasterCard, VISA, Discover, and American Express.